Blessed Is She

Blessed Is She
Living Lent with Mary

TIM PERRY

MOREHOUSE PUBLISHING

HARRISBURG / PENNSYLVANIA

Unless otherwise noted, the Scripture quotations contained herein are from the New Revised Standard Version Bible, copyright © 1989 by the Division of Christian Education of the National Council of Churches of Christ in the U.S.A. Used by permission. All rights reserved.

Morehouse Publishing, 4775 Linglestown Road, Harrisburg, PA 17112
Morehouse Publishing, 445 Fifth Ave., New York, NY 10016

Morehouse Publishing is an imprint of Church Publishing Incorporated.

Cover: *Pieta* by Jim Hasse, courtesy of Claver Jesuit Community,
        Cincinnati, Ohio
Cover design by Lee Singer
Page design by Beth Oberholtzer

Library of Congress Cataloging-in-Publication Data

Perry, Tim S., 1969 -
        Blessed is she : living Lent with Mary / Tim Perry.
            p.   cm.
        ISBN-13: 978-0-8192-2233-6 (pbk.)
        ISBN-10: 0-8192-2233-X (pbk.)
            1. Lent.   2. Mary, Blessed Virgin, Saint.   1. Title.
BV85.P54   2006
232.91—dc22

2006032625

Printed in the United States of America
07 08 09 10 9 8 7 6 5 4 3 2

This book is dedicated to the three most precious gifts
Rachel and I have received—Calvin, Sara and Hugh,
that they may with Mary say, "Let it be to me."

Greetings, blessed mother of Jesus
Heaven and earth's Ave be to you.
Let me after mute ages return
Before you to offer belated praise to your fame.

John Gwili Jenkins, *Wales and the Virgin Mary*[1]

Beautiful she is, sir! Lovely! Sometimes like a great
tree in flower, sometimes like a white daffadowndilly,
small and slender like. Hard as di'monds,
soft as moonlight. Warm as sunlight,
cold as frost in the stars. Proud and far-off
as a snow mountain, and as merry as any lass
I ever saw with daisies in her hair in springtime.

Sam Gamgee, *The Lord of the Rings*[2]

---

1. Quoted in Timothy George, "The Blessed Virgin Mary in Evangelical Perspective," in *Mary: Mother of God*, ed. Carl E. Braaten and Robert W. Jenson (Grand Rapids, MI: Eerdmans, 2004), 121.

2. J. R. R. Tolkien, *The Two Towers* (London: HarperCollins, 1994 [1966]), 357.

Contents

Acknowledgments

This book began as a series of sermons delivered during Lent, 2003 to the congregation of Saint Margaret's Anglican Church in Winnipeg, Manitoba, Canada. I am grateful to my pastor, the Rev. Dr. David Widdicombe, and to all in the vestry and congregation who thought these sermons deserved a wider audience and encouraged me to transcribe and develop them. I wish also to thank the Board and Cabinet of Providence College in Otterburne, Manitoba, Canada, for granting me a sabbatical during which this book took shape. Finally, my editor at Morehouse, Nancy Fitzgerald, a doctor skilled in curing the most difficult cases of "academitis," has earned my gratitude for her patience and sound advice.

A Lenten Mary
Mary as Model Disciple in Luke's Gospel

My soul doth magnify the Lord,
And my spirit hath rejoiced in God my Savior.
For he hath regarded
the lowliness of his handmaiden:
for, behold, from henceforth all generations
shall call me blessed.
(Luke 1:46b–48, KJV)

"The Magnificat" (Luke 1:46–56) is Mary's song of praise to God, a response to the extraordinary events that overtook what was once an ordinary life. When we meet her in Luke's Gospel, Mary is a teenager in Palestine, neither remarkably pious nor well-connected, a woman, a member of an oppressed people, probably illiterate, living in a rural backwater of the mighty Roman Empire. Then, apparently without warning, this very average young woman encounters a heavenly messenger named Gabriel who announces that she has been chosen to be the mother of the Savior of the world.

Mary is confused and troubled. No wonder. In response to her question, "How can this be?" the angel doesn't offer an explanation.

He says only that a sign—the unlikely pregnancy of Mary's aged cousin, Elizabeth—will confirm that his announcement is true. Was she confident, courageous, fearful, frantic, when she left her home and hurried to the hills, to Elizabeth's home? We don't know. Mary's mind—at this stage of the story, at least—is closed to us. We do know that Mary confirms the angel's words when she meets her cousin, the soon-to-be mother of John the Baptizer. We know that she receives her cousin's blessing. Only then does she give us her own insight, her own song.

It's the song of someone consciously caught up in a larger story— the story of God's faithfulness to God's people. If Mary is to be called the Blessed One by future generations, then it's only because God has—through her—kept the promises he made to her forefathers and -mothers.

And when we sing or chant Mary's words after her—in my own tradition, they are part of Evening Prayer—both her story and her song become our own. Like her, we become caught up in the story of God's gracious dealings with people. Each time we sing the Magnificat we are, or at least ought to be, filled with the same sense of wonder and joy that Mary must have felt. Each time we sing it, we want to rush out with Elizabeth to bless both the mother and the little one she carries. When we repeat Mary's declaration that all future generations will bless her, we become those who look to her, honor her memory, and bless her name. With Mary, we become a part of the gospel story, now no longer past, but living and active in us and in our words.

Incorporated into the gospel in this way, we have a closer relationship to Mary than we might at first realize. For many of us—including Christians with strong traditions of Marian devotion—Mary is a remote figure. She's almost lost, sometimes because two thousand years of history gets in the way—what could we possibly have in common with a first-century Jewish teenager? Sometimes she's just as remote because she's too transcendent, too near the divine, to be approachable—after all, what do any of us have in common with the Virgin Mother, the Mother of God?

When we, men and women, read the biblical text, however, we encounter a young woman who is neither historically distant nor a near-goddess. She is a real woman caught up in an unreal miracle. She is a woman who trusts, obeys, doubts, worries, ponders, and perseveres in the midst of the strangest of circumstances. Insofar as her story is one of starts and stops, moments of insight interrupting spans of ambiguity and ignorance, her story is deeply familiar to even the most "postmodern" Christian. Mary's life continues to speak across centuries to contemporary Christians. Today, her life continues to invite reflection and imitation.

Although this is true year round, it is especially so during Lent. This observation may not seem evident at first glance. Lent—the solemn period of fasting preceding Holy Week and Easter—is a time when believers prepare to remember and reenact the climax of Jesus' life: his suffering, death, and resurrection. The focus is not simply on Jesus taking up his cross, but also on us, and our own crosses—whatever they may be—in imitation of his devotion and obedience to God, his courageous and determined embrace of God's plan regardless of the personal cost.

Mary, on the other hand, is most obvious during the seasons of Advent, Christmas, and Epiphany. After all, in the Gospels of Matthew and Luke, her story is the story of the conception and birth of the Savior. Her role in both the birth stories is clearly defined by her relationship to Jesus. She is his mother. Even in those few places in the Gospels where she's mentioned, she doesn't have standing in her own right as much as she does as the mother of the Lord. As a result, Christians are often quite comfortable with Mary at the Christmas crèche, but unsure what to do with her after Epiphany. In the Gospels and in our piety, she fades into the background as Jesus assumes center stage.

I believe that this understanding is sound; I also believe that it is incomplete. When we read Mary's story as it's told in the Gospel of Luke closely, we find that it doesn't easily fit into Christmas confines. It belongs there, to be sure. But it quickly transcends those limits. For in Luke, Mary is not an afterthought—an "after all, *somebody* had to be Jesus' mother." She listens, speaks, acts, and decides. Luke's Mary doesn't stand in the shadow of Joseph, her husband; he stands in hers. When her baby is born and the new family present themselves at the temple, an elderly prophet, Simeon, recognizes the child as the Messiah and, ignoring convention, speaks directly to Mary rather than to her husband. Twelve years later, when the distraught parents find Jesus teaching in the temple, Mary—not her husband—chastises the child.

Again and again in the opening chapters of this Gospel, Mary is the central character. She's neither a model virgin, nor a model woman, but a model disciple who points all disciples—men and women alike—to a deep understanding of what discipleship really means. She is a Mary who belongs in Lent as much as in Advent, a Mary who shows what it means to die and live with the crucified and risen Jesus.

Drawing primarily—though not exclusively—on the Gospel of Luke, this book sketches a Lenten Mary, a Mary who teaches us about being a disciple. The first two chapters reflect on the annunciation, beginning with the angel's announcement that Mary has found favor with God. The angel offers no explanation for the divine gift. The announcement is as unexpected as it is bold. This is the radical and free nature of grace. And just as it came to Mary, so it comes to us: unbidden and unstoppable, drawing us into life with God. To be a disciple with Mary is to be chosen by God.

From the stunning announcement we move on to Mary's acceptance of the angel's call. Mary has been chosen; Mary freely affirms God's choice. To be a disciple with Mary is to recognize that disciples both work out their salvation with fear and trembling and acknowledge that this very work of dying and living with Christ is the work of God in us.

The next two chapters turn to the story of Elizabeth and Mary, starting with Elizabeth's double pronouncement of blessing. Mary, Elizabeth tells us, is blessed because of her child and because she believed. She is the Christian disciple living by faith alone. Uncertain of the future, she entrusts herself and her future to the One who has planned it. Mary is a model of what it means to trust completely in God.

Then we'll explore the Magnificat, Mary's song of response to her cousin's blessing, and its praise of a God who is always on the side of the poor, challenging the accepted notions of "the way things are." To be a disciple with Mary is to watch for such signs of God's presence in unexpected places.

The following two chapters move to the stories of Jesus' birth and presentation at the temple. While the shepherds rejoice at the amazing sights and sounds in the heavens, and others marvel at their tale, Mary silently broods. She understands some things, but much about herself and her son's destiny remains shrouded in mystery. So it is for all of us who follow Jesus. At points in our journey to the cross and resurrection with Jesus, the road—ahead and behind—will be clear. At other times the future will seem uncertain, hidden, perhaps even utterly irrational. What then? Mary's silence may provide direction.

We'll also attend to Simeon's warning, a warning that ties Mary's destiny to that of Jesus. Mary's son, says Simeon, will cause the rise and fall of many. He will provoke opposition that will expose the deepest thoughts of friend and foe alike. And Mary's heart will also be pierced. We find in Mary a disciple acquainted with the cost of redemption, whose example helps us understand our own suffering.

The last two chapters depart from Luke's Gospel. Only John places Mary at the foot of the cross on Good Friday. There, we meet a woman presented in a very different light, but one who—even at the darkest of times—is still an example to all her Son's followers. Finally, the sequel to Luke's Gospel, the Acts of the Apostles, lists Mary among those disciples who awaited the coming of the Holy

Spirit at Pentecost. At the cross and in the upper room, she is an example of perseverance.

No Christmas card sentimentality, no nativity scene no matter how intricate, can do justice to Mary as she is presented in the Gospel of Luke and elsewhere. She is the first follower of Jesus, a model for us all. As the season of Lent unfolds, let us learn together what it means to bless Mary, and in so doing, come better to love her son—her Savior and ours—as we learn the way of dying and living to which Jesus calls us.

This book is an invitation to turn to Mary this Lent. It follows a simple format. Each chapter begins by listing the biblical passage and quoting the key verse on which it is based; each ends with a short prayer and a list of questions designed to stimulate learning whether through group discussion or individual reflection. Each aims to invite readers to place themselves inside the biblical story and to let that story shed new light on their own. With Mary, let's engage in the disciplines of listening, discerning, and applying the Divine Word as it comes to us couched in the human words of Holy Scripture. Her story reveals the core of our Christian faith. Her character shows us what a faith-full response to that core looks like. Her life shows us what our own devotion to Jesus should resemble.

> O Lord Jesus Christ,
> who took up our humanity in the womb of Mary,
> to redeem it:
> we would follow her example
> and offer ourselves, our souls and bodies, wholly to your care;
> so that we, through it, may better love and praise your
>   holy name.
> O blessed Savior, grant this we pray
> for your own name's sake.
> Amen.

∽ LENT 1 ∾

You Have Found Favor
The Mystery of Grace

LUKE 1:5–38

"And the angel said unto her, Fear not,
Mary: for thou hast found favor with God"
(Luke 1:30, KJV)

How does the lifelong journey of discipleship that's condensed and intensified in Lent begin? That's the first question we'll look at together. But before sketching an answer, however, let's be clear on what this journey involves. Here's a definition that will guide us throughout the following chapters: Becoming a disciple involves coming to understand, own, and live the gospel—that is, the good news that God has acted in Jesus to save us.

It's an ongoing navigation between two poles. The negative pole is what the Christian tradition has called "mortification," that is, "putting to death" those parts of our selves that don't conform God's will as it's disclosed in the Bible. Discipleship (in part) is a lifetime of unlearning those attitudes and habits that come all too naturally to fallen human beings, that appear so natural and wholesome, that are so enslaving.

The positive pole, "vivification," is just the opposite. It's the slow process of being "made alive" in and through Christ. It's the Holy

Spirit-enabled and directed practicing of those habits and virtues through which our minds are renewed, our bodies controlled, our selves transformed. It's a process through which our consciences become guided by principles like moderation, patience, and generosity as we learn to love God with our whole hearts, our neighbors as ourselves, and within the boundaries of such love, to enjoy the gifts of God's creation.

Finally, this journey of dying and living is one that we take with others, beginning and ending in community. Becoming Christ's disciple begins and ends with sisters and brothers alongside us, struggling with us, bearing our burdens as we bear theirs, forgiving and being forgiven, praying with us, for us, and perhaps sometimes instead of us. It's a journey undertaken in and with the Church as the Church hears in Word and sees in Sacrament God's promise and command.

With that in mind, we turn to the text that will occupy us for the next two chapters: the angel Gabriel's announcement that Mary is to be Jesus' mother. First, an overview: although Mary is present only in the opening two chapters of Luke's Gospel, there, she is central. This is unique among the New Testament's four Gospels. In the earliest and shortest Gospel, Mark, Mary is mentioned by name only once, and in her only appearance she is in fact one of Jesus' opponents.

In Matthew's Gospel, oriented as it is toward Jewish Christians, Mary is passive, caught up in the events that revolve around Joseph, who is the main character of the opening chapters. We may even say that the scandalous situation in which she finds herself—unmarried and pregnant—is the focal point of conflict early on in Matthew's narrative. It's both an obstacle that only God can at once account for and remove, and a foil against which Joseph, the righteous servant of God, displays his upright character.

The Gospel of John is totally different again: never named, the mother of Jesus appears at a wedding where water is transformed into wine (chapter 2) and at the cross when Jesus' mission is accomplished (chapter 19). In this Gospel, the anonymous woman is lost in the symbolic way she's tied to the coming of what John calls "Jesus' hour." At the wedding she is present when the hour hasn't come; at the cross she's present when the hour arrives. Mary ties both scenes together.

Even though much of Luke's Gospel closely resembles Matthew and Mark, his portrait of Mary is different yet again. His Mary is the most sharply drawn of several characters—Gentiles, women, children, and the poor—who didn't fit easily in proper Jewish society. In Luke, stories and descriptions involving these kinds of people are always significant and sympathetic. Luke wants us to notice and to feel for them *because* they're on the margins of the community of faith. His Gospel isn't for saints, but for sinners.

Luke's audience—embodied in a character named Theophilus, to whom the story is addressed—is made up of people attracted to Jesus' words and example, but conscious of their place on the periphery of organized faith. Luke has good news for these people whose relationship to God is unclear, whether they live among God's chosen people (such as the shepherds in Luke 2) or are obvious yet sympathetic outsiders (such as the faith-filled Roman officer of Luke 7).

Mary, a young, single woman with a pregnancy that would have provoked questions, is one of those people on the margins. She's one of God's people who appears to almost all to be trapped by social convention in a scandalous situation. Only she and Elizabeth apparently know that what looks like scandal is, in fact, the greatest of all miracles. From this perspective, Mary truly is a three-dimensional character. Only here is she in the narrative's foreground, the one around whom the conflict seems to revolve.

She's introduced in Luke's second announcement story, which opens with the words, "In the sixth month" (1:26). Were we simply to jump in there, we might conclude that this refers to the sixth month of the year, but we'd be wrong. As Luke makes clear a few verses later (1:36), the "sixth month" refers not to a calendar but to Elizabeth's pregnancy. Luke uses this little phrase to tie Mary's story to the first announcement story: Gabriel's announcement that Zechariah and Elizabeth are soon to become the parents of John the Baptizer (1:5–25). To understand Mary's story, we must begin with Zechariah and Elizabeth's.

Luke's first announcement story is full of rich allusions to the Old Testament, found in even the plainest of phrases. Consider the opening: "It happened in the days of Herod, King of Judea." At first glance, this looks like a straightforward way to anchor Luke's story in everyday history. When we look deeper, though, we find that Luke uses it also to ground his story in biblical history.

These opening words look very much like the opening verses of the Old Testament prophetic books Jeremiah (1:2, 3) and Amos (1:1), a resemblance that's both deliberate and significant. It's a technique for Luke to situate his story in two ways. First, he signals to his readers that his story happens in the real world—their world—and not in one of the many legendary worlds of Greek mythology. Second, he invites readers to anticipate that the story will be about a mighty act of God similar to those in the Old Testament, from the days of the kings and prophets.

Moving past this introduction, there are even more hints of older biblical stories in the way the main characters are described. The couple, Luke tells us, is childless—Elizabeth is barren and both she and Zechariah are old. What a sparse description! And yet, to an imagination familiar with the story of Scripture, these few words offer a rich and compelling image. For through them, Luke has mentioned at least five sets of biblical parents whose children are major characters in the corporate life of God's people. And recalling their stories helps us understand the significance of what's to come.

Zechariah and Elizabeth's predicament calls to mind a narrative theme that runs through the Old Testament, in which God miraculously compensates for age and infertility. Standing behind this old, barren couple Luke intends for us to see, first and foremost, Abraham and Sarah (Gen 18:11). Of course, Isaac and Rebekah (Gen 25:21) and Jacob and Rachel (Gen 29:31) are also there, as are Manoah and his anonymous wife (Judg 13), and Elkannah and Hannah (1 Sam 1).

But the place of these parents in Jewish history is unrivalled not simply because of their extraordinary conceptions but also because the children conceived went on to serve God and God's people in powerful ways. They were chosen by God to advance God's plan for God's people. Abraham and Sarah bore Isaac, the "son of the promise," through whom Abraham would become a nation that in turn would bless the world. Rebekah became the mother of Jacob, who lent his name, Israel, to an entire nation; Rachel, Jacob's favorite wife, gave birth to one of that nation's twelve tribes, Benjamin, and was grandmother to two more, Ephraim and Mannaseh. And though she's never given a name of her own, Manoah's wife gave birth to Samson, the strong man who saved the Israelites from their enemies, the Philistines. Elkannah and Hannah, finally, were the parents of Samuel, Israel's last and greatest judge. And Samuel, in turn, instituted the monarchy, anointing not only Israel's first king, Saul, but also its greatest king, David.

In just that one sentence, Luke shows his audience that his characters aren't simply historical or literary devices. Instead, they stand at the end of a long line of biblical history. Through just a few words, Luke tells his readers that his story isn't new. So when they meet Zechariah and Elizabeth, they understand that the next chapter in the story of God's dealings with Israel and the human race has begun.

The Old Testament traces continue as the plot unfolds. Zechariah's encounter with the angel in the temple appears to draw from two streams. The first stream is the commission of the prophet Isaiah to take what would prove to be an unpopular message to the people (Isa 6:1–13). But where Isaiah's message would lead to judgment, John's would lead to restoration. The second stream flows from the book of the Prophet Daniel, in the repeated name of the angel

Gabriel. This is no accident. Gabriel is named only four times in the Christian Bible—twice in Daniel (8:16; 9:21) and twice in Luke (1:19, 26). Gabriel is that angelic messenger charged with interpreting Daniel's visions about the end time. His presence in Luke's Gospel signals that what was future for Daniel is now present. In the ministries of John and Jesus, the Day of the Lord has come.

And Gabriel's description of John likens him to two or three great biblical figures. Like Samson the judge, John will take the vows of a Nazirite, abstaining from alcohol (compare Judges 13:7 and Luke 1:15). Like Elijah the prophet, he will teach the people (compare Malachi 4:5–6 and Luke 1:17). John himself will stand in a line of judges and prophets sent by God to God's people to herald their salvation.

And Zechariah's response to Gabriel's strange declaration reminds readers of Abraham. When God promises Abraham that he'll have an heir of his own, a physical son who himself is but the beginning of numberless descendants, as well as a land in which these descendants will live, Abraham's question is shockingly blunt: "How am I to know?" (Gen 15:8). Similarly, having heard Gabriel's announcement, Zechariah recovers from his initial terror enough to ask, "How will I know that this is so?" (Luke 1:18). Both the patriarch and the priest seek certainty before they trust in God's promise.

Finally, when Elizabeth finds that she is pregnant, she withdraws from public life with these words: "This is what the Lord has done for me when he looked favorably on me and took away the disgrace I have endured among my people" (Luke 1:25). Her declaration recalls not only the similar situation of Sarah (Gen 21:1), but also the very words of Rachel at the birth of her son, Joseph: "God has taken away my reproach" (Gen 30:23).

Luke peppers his story with references to the stories of the people of Israel, and that communicates two ideas. First, *God* is acting again. Readers shouldn't be surprised by John's arrival—after all,

God has done similar things in the past. Second, God is acting *in the same way* as in the past. Throughout the history of the Hebrew people, God made promises and brought them to fulfillment, sometimes in miraculous ways. God is doing the same here.

Luke's second announcement story seems at first like a continuation of the first one. In both, the main characters are introduced: Zechariah and Elizabeth (1:5) and Mary (1:27). Next, a condition preventing conception is described: Zechariah and Elizabeth were old (1:7) and Mary is a virgin (1:27). Both Zechariah and Mary are "troubled" by the angel's sudden appearance (1:12; 29). Gabriel calls both characters by name and offers them words of comfort (1:13; 30). Both announcements follow the same pattern: a child's birth is predicted, his name is given, his future is foretold, and the role of the Holy Spirit is described (1:13–17; 30–33). Both Zechariah and Mary question Gabriel's words and receive a sign, and then Gabriel departs (1:18–22; 34–38). These aren't accidental intersections; there are just too many of them.

But despite the parallels that pull us into the two stories, a new list of contrasts exposes the uniqueness of the second one. First, look at Gabriel's words to Mary. His announcement to Zechariah is a response to prayer (1:13). His announcement to Mary, on the other hand, comes from out of the blue—entirely by divine initiative (1:28). Elizabeth's conception is like a miracle of healing and is foreshadowed in the infertile parents of the Old Testament. Mary's, however, is without biblical precedent and is better understood as a miracle of creation. Gabriel greets Zechariah by name; but for Mary, adds the title, "Favored One."

Then there are the sharp contrasts between the promised children. John, we are told, will be great in God's sight (1:15). Jesus' greatness is unqualified (1:32). John would be made holy by his vows (1:15). Jesus, says Gabriel, will be holy from conception (1:35). John will prepare the way of the Lord (1:16–17). Jesus will reign on

David's throne as the Son of God (1:32; 35). John is filled with the Spirit from his conception (1:15). Jesus' very existence is by the power of the Spirit alone (1:35). The contrasts clearly intend to highlight the relationship between John and Jesus as that of herald to King. The former comes as the King's representative, a vitally important—but only preparatory—role. Having prepared the way and the people, when the King comes, his mission is completed. John, though older, will serve his younger cousin.

The main characters are also different. Zechariah is a priest; Elizabeth descends from the line of priests. They are old, married, righteous and childless. Taken together, these qualities mark them as exceptional. The reason is simple: God should have rewarded an old, priestly, righteous couple with many children and even grandchildren for their piety and obedience. Their childlessness doesn't fit the Old Testament ideal of an upright married life blessed by God. That they haven't been so blessed is a public disgrace and a reproach because it calls into question whether the apparent righteousness of this couple is, in fact, true. Without children, it will always be possible for their neighbors to wonder whether Zechariah's and Elizabeth's holiness is a sham.

Now look at Mary. She is obviously not a priest and, though Elizabeth's cousin, her lineage is unclear. Where Zechariah and Elizabeth stand out as part of the deep biblical tradition of infertile parents, everything about Mary is, well, normal and nondescript. She's young, engaged, not renowned for her piety, and (presumably) fertile. And yet it's Zechariah who can't believe the announcement (1:18), while Mary declares herself ready to be a part of the divine plan (1:38).

Luke opens his Gospel with two stories with two sets of parallels—one linking, the other contrasting. On the one hand, the similarities are clearly designed to show that the God who opened the wombs of Sarah, of Rachel and Rebekah, of Manoah's wife, and of Hannah is acting again, both in Elizabeth and in Mary. In the Old Testament, God miraculously compensated for barrenness and age, so that special sons might be conceived and born in the usual way: Isaac, Jacob, Joseph and Benjamin, Samson, and Samuel. Both John the Baptizer and Jesus stand together in the Bible's tradition of improbable pregnancies, promised sons, and the fulfillment of God's plan.

On the other hand, something new is going on with Mary, setting her apart from both Elizabeth and the other famous Old Testament mothers. But Luke doesn't tell us what it is. When he records Gabriel's greeting, "Greetings, favored one! The Lord is with you!" (1:28), Luke wants us to be baffled. Is there something about Mary we don't know? What has she done to deserve God's favor? Who is she to have merited such a title?

As we read on, it's clear we aren't the only ones who are surprised. Mary herself is troubled and confused by Gabriel's words. Yet when he speaks again, he offers no explanation for the title. He says, "Do not be afraid, Mary, for you have found favor with God" (1:30). In other words, Mary is the Favored One simply because she's the recipient of God's favor. That's no explanation at all! Although Mary may well have been calmed by the angel's second speech, her confusion (and ours) only grows. Then the angel continues. Mary will conceive a son. She will name him Jesus. He will be called the Son of God and reign on his father David's throne forever. "How can this be," responds the bewildered girl, "since I am a virgin?" (1:34).

Let's consider these two points. First, Mary's question offers a glimpse into her mind-set. In the previous story, Zechariah seems content to believe in the possibility of a miracle, with sufficient evidence that Gabriel was a trustworthy source of information. His question, in other words, reveals a skeptical or doubtful attitude. But Mary's question is quite different. It presumes the reliability of the announcement and, based on that presumption, wonders how things will work out. Her "how is this possible?" far from indicating disbelief, in fact reveals her deep trust.

Second, Mary's question reveals a biological condition. Mary isn't simply young and engaged. She is a virgin, so it's impossible for her to conceive. Her question gives the angel an opening to disclose more information. This child's existence, says Gabriel, depends solely on God's Holy Spirit, and he offers Mary this sign: Your cousin Elizabeth has also conceived and is in her sixth month. Nothing is impossible with God.

Mary stands out from Elizabeth and the other Old Testament mothers precisely by not being special. As we meet her in Luke 1, she's thoroughly ordinary. There's no explanation for her being chosen to be the mother of the Lord. Mary is the recipient of the greatest of all graces for no reason other than that God is—and is determined to be—gracious. So it is that Mary's journey, which will later be heralded by angels and seen by shepherds, blessed by Simeon and Anna, filled with doubts and dangers, comes to its climax at the foot of a cross as her son hangs suspended between heaven and earth, begins with an announcement of God's favor. Mary's journey with Jesus to the cross and resurrection begins with grace.

And this is the moment to shift from Mary's world to ours. In Mary's story Luke conveys—then and now—a deep and liberating gospel truth: God's grace doesn't depend on our piety, prayer, or position in life.

This is perhaps the most difficult lesson of Lent to learn, given its quite natural focus on mortification and vivification—that putting to death of our old habits and attitudes coupled with the careful nurture of virtuous patterns of behavior and frames of mind. Lent's stress on disciplined behavior may lead us (mistakenly) to conclude that we are, in fact, engaged in an attempt to stake a claim for the gift of God's favor. The result is either one of two of the deadliest sins.

One is despair. The emphasis on holiness may lead some of us to conclude that we are not, have not been, and will never be good enough to receive God's grace. And if we can never earn it, why bother trying? We may conclude that grace isn't for us—maybe the repentance of Lent is best left to others. To those for whom this conclusion comes all too easily, Mary's story teaches that repentance is not the foundation for grace. Rather, grace is the ground of repentance.

Grace didn't come to Mary because of her social status, family line, or superior piety; grace came to Mary because God is gracious. This is the fundamental point of Gabriel's explanation that Mary is the Favored One because she has received God's favor: No other explanation can be given for no other is necessary. The point Luke intends the story to reveal is not something about Mary, but something about God. Luke deliberately turns our attention away from Mary and toward God, the God who lavishes his love and acceptance on people who cannot earn it.

Why should we repent? Why should we do things that remind us of our mortality, expose our sins, and call to mind just how far we have to go in our journeys of discipleship? For just one reason: In Christ, God has already chosen us to be the objects of his love. In baptism, God has, through the Holy Spirit, united us to Jesus Christ. God has made the destiny of Jesus our own.

This grace cannot be earned, only received. The words of the angel to Mary, in her ordinariness, are in fact words to us all: "Greetings, Favored One! The Lord is with you!" And if, like Mary, we ask in confusion, "How can this be?" we have the angel's assurance: "With God, nothing is impossible." Because grace has wholly to do with God's decision to be gracious, no one needs to lose their hope, indeed their selves, in despair.

But not all of us despair during Lent. It may be that, having accepted the mistaken notion that repentance comes before grace, some of us go on to commit despair's equal and opposite sin, pride— thinking that we're good enough, disciplined enough, and repentant enough to receive God's grace. God's favor is nothing other than the crowning achievement of our own efforts.

It may be that in deepest recesses of our hearts, we really do believe that God owes us for our piety, our prayers, our positions of religious respectability. And again, the example of Mary shows that this isn't so. Like her, we're on the margins, ordinary, frail, and needy. There's no room for pride when we recognize that discipline is a response to grace.

Mary's story reminds both the despairing and the proud that however painful the way of repentance is, it's founded on and determined by God's grace. And this is perhaps the greatest irony of all. Common sense assumes God's favor should lead to a comfortable life of relative wealth, security, and happiness. Mary, however, invites us to be skeptical. Her journey with Jesus didn't include physical prosperity. It didn't produce a happy family life. It didn't lead to a land of security and comfort for her or her people.

In fact, the Gospels suggest precisely the opposite. When they pull her from anonymity, they hint that Mary's life was one in which her son was not hers, but was devoted to God; one in which she wondered whether her son was mentally healthy; one in which others questioned her reputation and his parentage; one of political conflict that culminated in the cross. All because she was the Favored One. She who gave assent to God's plan for the world was given no guarantee. For in this world, there are none—not for any of us. There's only caution not to presume that wealth provides security and a promise that poverty doesn't keep the giver of grace from being generous. For Mary, as for us, grace comes first. That's the great mystery we can't exhaust. Either in despair or pride, we want to convince ourselves that we really are the authors of our own salvation and whether we succeed or fail, it's down to us. After all, doesn't the Bible say, "God helps those who help themselves"? No, actually, the Bible doesn't. The Bible says that God in Christ helps those who can't help themselves, that God in Christ frees those who are enslaved, that God in Christ raises corpses to new life, that God calls without favor, that God saves indiscriminately, that grace is for the worst of sinners. Sinners—we—are the objects of God's love. We are those on whom God's favor rests.

The journey to the cross is our journey, but more than that, it's the journey of God with us, a journey that begins and ends with the announcement that we are favored, that the Lord is with us, that we are blessed. And the only explanation we have is that this is so because this is who God is.

Almighty God,
who sent Gabriel to announce your favor
to Mary,
save us from despair and pride;
in order that we may repent fully and freely,
confident in the love with which you first loved us.
Grant this we pray
through Jesus Christ, Our Lord.
Amen.

For Reflection and Discussion

1. Discipleship is "coming to understand, own, and live the gospel." How is this kind of discipleship worked out in your church community? In your own life? How do these examples help you think about Lent?

2. For you, which is the most challenging aspect of discipleship— mortifying or vivifying? Why?

3. Re-read the stories of Zechariah and Elizabeth and Mary, paying particular attention to Luke's understanding of timing. Why, do you suppose, might Luke tie God's activity to the timing of Elizabeth's pregnancy, rather than, say, that of a calendar?

4. Is Gabriel's explanation that Mary is favored just because she is favored sufficient for you? Why or why not? Think about instances of grace in your own life. How are they like Mary's experience?

5. Do you struggle more with despair that you cannot earn God's grace, or pride in your conviction that you can? How does Luke's portrayal of grace as a radical and free gift challenge your thinking?

6. Grace is the foundation of repentance. What does this mean to you? Do you agree or disagree? Why?

Behold God's Slave

The Mystery of Freedom

LUKE 1:26–38

"Then Mary said, 'Here am I, the servant of the Lord;
let it be with me according to your word.'"

(Luke 1:38)

In the movie *The Truman Show*,[3] the comedic actor Jim Carrey plays the title character, Truman Burbank. Unbeknownst to him, Truman's life is completely scripted for a television show in which he is the central character. The town in which he lives (Seahaven), his job (insurance adjuster), and his home are all unreal. His best friend, Marlon, his high school sweetheart, Lauren, and his wife, Meryl are actors directed by Christof (played by Ed Harris). Even the traumatic death of his father (played by Brian Delate) in a sailing accident is merely a way of writing a troublesome actor out of the show while increasing ratings.

And the ratings are huge! In the fictional world of the movie, *The Truman Show* is the most popular TV program in history. The only thing larger than its audience is its advertising revenue. Millions of people are glued to their sets every week to see how Truman will

---

3. *The Truman Show*, directed by Peter Weir, Paramount Pictures, 1998.

respond to whatever situations Christof designs and throws his way. Truman is the only person not only in Seahaven but also, apparently, the television-viewing world who doesn't know that it's all a sham.

Through a series of small miscues, however, Truman begins to discover that the only world he's ever known is a façade. Indeed, he discovers to his horror that what he had for so many years taken to be "real life" is an immaculately groomed, safe, and pleasant prison. There are no obvious signs of abuse. Truman has a job he seems to enjoy, a wife who apparently loves him, a best friend who has displayed unswerving loyalty since childhood. In many ways, his life is enviable! And yet, no matter how agreeable it is, Truman eventually discovers that he'll never really be free to live as long as he's under Christof's control. A life in which every contingency is planned out in advance, in which every outcome is scripted beforehand, is an unreal life. An un-free life.

Once he overcomes the shock of his discovery, Truman resolves to escape to the real world. At the climax of the movie, Truman embarks on a voyage to the end of the world. Although his first attempts to leave Seahaven are foiled, he finally steers his sailboat, the *Santa Maria* (aptly named for another vessel that once sailed to the world's edge) through a life-threatening storm to the horizon—which is to say, the back wall of the television studio in which he's lived his entire life.

Until now, Christof has remained behind the scenes, pulling the strings. Although invisible, he deliberately places various obstacles in Truman's way, hoping at all costs (and given the advertising revenue, they are huge) to prevent Truman's voyage of discovery and the end of the program. Truman, however, is determined. If Christof is to maintain control, he must reveal himself. After years of behind-the-scenes maneuvering, he must intervene directly in Truman's life. Speaking from the control room (Truman's moon), Christof tells Truman that he has a simple decision to make. He can either continue to live in his sealed environment—same job, same wife, same friends, with all his needs cared for—or he can leave for a world full of unknowns. Truman knows that however tempting an offer this is, he will never experience true love, true friendship, and true happiness in a world where all risks of loss are removed. He declines the offer with a smile, gropes his way to a door hidden on the horizon, and, with a final "Good afternoon, good evening, and good night!" exits.

All along, the film's audience has been carefully positioned to cheer for Truman by showing how his process of discovery has captured the imaginations of his fictional TV viewers. They are the vehicle through which director Peter Weir enables us to suspend our disbelief, to come to care for Truman, for his well-being, and for his eventual success. Having created this bond, both the fictional and real audiences are caught up in Truman's voyage to freedom so that when he rejects Christof, they and we both cheer. (At least, when I first saw the movie, onscreen cheers were matched in the cinema.)

Although the movie ends with the rolling of the credits, Truman's story does not. We are left with the feeling that it's just begun. Will it hold joy? Sorrow? Will he reunite with the only woman who ever loved him? Will their love form the basis of a lasting relationship? How will Truman respond to his first real experience of loss or grief? None of these questions is answered. The director has left the audience knowing only that now Truman is in control of his life. Christof's direction has been left behind forever. Truman is free. His life will run the course that he chooses.

For me, the movie is both fascinating and disturbing, for it says a great deal on at least three levels. On the surface, it's a surreal tale made believable by superb direction, acting, and our own cultural fascination with so-called reality TV. Not only is it a compelling and well-told story, but in a pop-culture defined at least in part by *Survivor*, *Big Brother*, and *The Apprentice*, it's increasingly easy for the audience to get involved. With the announcement of each new fall programming season, *The Truman Show* becomes just a little more plausible.

There's more to this movie, however, than an exposé of the extremes of reality TV. Just beneath this surface, *The Truman Show* is a scathing indictment of the ways the popular culture of North America can and does assess the pain and joys of real life according to their entertainment value.

The immoral roots of this "if it bleeds, it leads" attitude are laid bare when it seems Truman's desire to escape will be frustrated finally only by his death. When this is raised as a possibility, an unnamed network executive with just a shred of a conscience left shouts, "For God's sake, Chris! The whole world is watching. We can't let him die in front of a live audience!" Christof—any pretense to morality lost in the quest for bigger ratings and larger profits—coolly replies, "He was born in front of a live audience." One wonders which is more shocking: Christof's amoral assessment of the situation, or just how plausible the entire onscreen conversation seems to those of us trapped in the twenty-four-hour news cycle.

The Truman Show is a superb piece of social commentary, both as an indictment of reality TV and of the larger everything-is-entertainment culture that spawned it. And had these been the director's main goals, the movie ought still to be recognized as a fine work of art. But we still haven't got to the core issues explored in the movie. These are neither cultural nor social, but theological. They have to do with what appear (at least in Peter Weir's eyes) to be mutually exclusive claims: on the one hand, God exists and on the other, human beings are free. Weir provocatively suggests that for one claim to be true, the other must be false. And it's clear which claim he would have us relinquish: God.

So the film is a dramatization of the theological argument that has defined our age more than any other. It's a debate that, though it's more than two hundred years old, seems never to lose its freshness or power. From the beginning of the Age of Enlightenment to today, many intellectuals have come to the conclusion that human beings can never truly be themselves and can never be free until they rid themselves of the illusion of an all-powerful God. While such a belief system may have been inevitable and indeed necessary in the early stages of social development, runs one version of the argument, now human society has matured to the level that it can safely be left behind. An adult attitude toward God is essentially the same as one toward Santa Claus: we may from time to time look back with a sense of nostalgia for innocence lost, but never ever with regret.

A fresh take on this debate is offered by the source of conflict in this film—the acknowledgement that Truman (True Man?) can never become a fully free, fully responsible human agent as long as Christof (Christ?) offers safety in exchange for control and treats him like a child, a puppet—invites viewers to enter into this debate anew. It bids us to ask what it takes to be truly free, to be an authentic human being, in such a sympathetic way that many fail to realize that it offers its own answer. And that answer is straightforward: a universe without God—or at least without a God who interferes in people's lives.

Luke's story of the annunciation may well, at least for a contemporary reader, provoke the same question. After all, Mary hasn't had much of a say, has she? Gabriel shows up without invitation, greets without explanation, and announces without preparation. How is Mary free in all this? And Mary's response hardly helps, for through it Luke insists that the believer's true freedom is found only in slavery to God.

The Truman Show and the Annunciation invite similar questions and suggest totally different answers. And for us, Luke and Mary's answer is the harder sell. The notion that authentic human freedom is found only in submission to God is a claim that runs counter to the most deeply held value in North America—that, in the words of the poem "Invictus," "I am the master of my fate and the captain of my soul." Yet it's a claim that runs to the heart of Christian discipleship. So let's consider it carefully.

Let's begin with a short re-cap. In chapter one, we were with Mary as she heard the words of the angel, Gabriel. We saw Luke contrast Mary with Zechariah and Elizabeth by showing the parallels between their angelic announcements of miraculous conceptions. Unlike Zechariah and Elizabeth, and all the characters in the Old Testament tradition of miraculous births in which they stand, Mary is unique. And, in a wonderful example of Luke's irony, she is so precisely by being ordinary.

There's nothing about Luke's description of her that explains her status as God's Favored One. There's nothing in her person, in her position, or in her piety that remotely suggests that she has earned her place in God's plan. When the angel Gabriel hails her as blessed among women, she is as baffled as everyone else. When the angel outlines God's plan, Mary is even more confused: "How can I, a virgin, conceive a child?" she asks. The angel's explanation isn't very satisfactory. Mary will conceive through the miraculous, creative work of the Holy Spirit, for nothing is impossible with God.

Mary's experience of God's lavish, overwhelming—and indeed irresistible—grace is a model for all Luke's readers. As it was for Mary, so it is for us: God's gracious gift of his presence does not depend on any previous assessment of our person, position, or piety. So there's no room in the Christian life for despair—as though we have excluded ourselves from grace, or pride—as though we've merited it. There's only room for thanksgiving to God in Christ, who freely pours out his grace on us.

As we move on in this chapter to the conclusion of the annunciation story, some people may wish that it had ended with Gabriel's words and that Mary's response would have forever been lost. Maybe you're like me and find yourself wanting to rewrite Luke's story to move straight from Gabriel's announcement of a miraculous conception to Mary to the announcement of the birth of the Messiah to terrified shepherds. For Mary's answer to Gabriel and to God doesn't rest easy on the ears of enlightened, postmodern, egalitarian, North American Christians. Her words don't comfort. Rather, they confront. They challenge. They make readers wince. For Mary acknowledges the angel's announcement and accepts God's call with the words, "Behold God's slave! May it be to me as you have spoken."[4]

What? She can't say that! Her words seems subtly to approve of the idea that human beings can be bought and sold like cows or chairs. We may recall to our collective shame the version of race-based slavery that fuelled the economies of the British Empire until 1832 and the southern plantations in the United States until the Civil War. While it may well be true that the Bible, though it didn't condone slavery, seemed simply to accept it as a fact of social life, the versions of slavery common to its cultures were never based on the morally and spiritually reprehensible notion that some human beings were in all ways superior to others.

And yet, some Christians justified the practice as God's curse on the descendents of Ham. According to the biblical tale, the descendants of Ham were cursed forever to serve the descendants of his brothers, Shem and Japheth, because Ham either participated in, passively permitted, or at least gossiped about his father's illicit sexual activity (see Gen 9:18–28).[5] Over centuries of biblical interpretation, Ham came to be seen as the progenitor of black Africans, a reading employed by nineteenth-century slave holders (and twentieth-century segregationists) to provide biblical support for their reprehensible views and actions.[6]

Neither can we soothe our consciences that such views were common only to relatively few, relatively uneducated people who wound up on the wrong side of the debate. For we may also remember with astonishment the story of Dred Scott, who, with his wife Harriet, sued his mistress, Irene Emerson, for his freedom in the St. Louis circuit

---

4. The word *doulé* is translated as "servant" in English Bibles (but not in translations of nonbiblical literature). "Slave," however, is a more accurate translation, and my own from the Greek text.

5. The Hebrew grammar of the verse makes the precise nature of Ham's sin unclear. Whatever its particulars, it is regarded by the Bible as irredeemable.

6. An excellent treatment of the issue is Stephen R. Haynes' book, *Noah's Curse: The Biblical Justification of American Slavery* (Oxford: Oxford University Press, 2002).

court in 1846. After a decade of legal challenges and appeals, the case finally went to the United States Supreme Court in 1857. In *Scott v. Sanford*, the court made two conclusions. First, Dred Scott as a slave was not a citizen of the United States and therefore not entitled to a citizen's right to liberty; second, as a slave, he was personal property and never had been free. God save this honorable court, indeed!

Fortunately, the same Christian faith that was abused by some to underwrite slavery was also the impetus behind the abolitionist movement both in Britain and in North America. Finally, we recall the courage of an aged Anglican priest, John Wesley, who, in 1791, dictated his final letter to a young Member of Parliament, William Wilberforce:

> Dear Sir: Unless the divine power has raised you up . . . I see not how you can go through your glorious enterprise in opposing that execrable villainy which is the scandal of religion, of England, and of human nature. Unless God has raised you up for this very thing, you will be worn out by the opposition of men and devils. But if God be for you, who can be against you? Are all of them together stronger than God? O be not weary of well doing! Go on, in the name of God and in the power of his might, till even American slavery (the vilest that ever saw the sun) shall vanish away before it.

And we may say with Abraham Lincoln and the radical wing of the Republican Party in the 1860s, "if slavery isn't wrong, then nothing is wrong!"

Given this checkered, all-too-long and all-too-recent history, it's understandable if some of us are embarrassed by Mary's words, "Behold God's slave." They seem not only to endorse this dark chapter in the history of Christendom, but also willingly to participate in and approve of it. Feminist theologians are right to observe that these words have created a perception of Mary as quietly compliant, an attitude to be emulated by too many in manifestly unjust situations. Her acceptance of slavery to the Lord could well have been used to authorize the treating of human beings as property and justify the oppression of women in general by men in general.

The difficulty may also be very personal. Mary's words may have been used to validate abusive patterns of evil racist or sexist behavior and speech that will forever prevent sisters (and brothers) from hearing them without pain. Slavery may be ended, but racist and sexist attitudes and behaviour continue to permeate at least segments of our society, poisoning minds, justifying abuse, horribly scarring God's creatures, both victims and perpetrators.

To deal seriously with these biblical words, we need to face honestly the cultural and personal challenges posed by the way they've been used. Unfortunately a major obstacle to such an honest encounter is presented by modern English translations of the Bible. The Greek word spoken by Mary in Luke's text is *doulé*, a form of the noun uniformly translated "slave" when it arises in non-biblical ancient literature. Curiously, in translations of the Bible, it's more often rendered "servant."

For example, the New International Version has Mary say, "I am the Lord's servant." Similarly, the New Revised Standard Version translates the phrase, "Here am I, the servant of the Lord." The Contemporary English Version, New Living Translation, New American Bible, and many others, have similar renderings. "Servant" doesn't sound like such an affront to the accepted moral axioms of our time. "Servant" is softer. "Servant" is safer. "Servant" is a poor translation.

The most straightforward English equivalent of *doulé* is not servant—someone who chooses to serve, but slave—someone who is chosen to serve. And that is the word Luke's Mary speaks. "Behold God's slave." Think those words through slowly. If they offend, let them offend. If they anger, let them anger. But most of all, let them be what they are. For it's with these words that Mary makes known that she clearly recognizes that God has chosen her and that she serves under that constraint. Don't allow her words to be softened by changing moral attitudes, even when those attitudes are right. For it's only when we allow Luke's Mary to speak in her own voice, to use her own words, that we begin to get a glimpse of just how powerful a character she is in Luke's Gospel and how she can serve as a model disciple for Lent and throughout the Church year.

The best place to begin if we are to interpret Mary's words rightly is not our own experience of slavery, but the rich biblical images that provide their natural context. If we attend to this and similar phrases in the New Testament book of Acts (Luke's sequel), it's clear that the words simply indicate Mary's willingness to serve God. In Acts, Luke applies it to women and men (Acts 2:18), believers generally (Acts 4:29), and to Paul and his companions (Acts 16:17). As far as Luke is concerned, "slave" describes all disciples, whether male or female, named or anonymous. This seems to indicate that Mary takes on this role not because of her sex or her inferiority, but simply because she recognizes God's call.

This conclusion is strengthened elsewhere in the New Testament. For instance, Paul speaks of himself as a "slave of Jesus Christ" (Rom 1:1) and describes all believers as "slaves to righteousness" (Rom 6:18). He even announces just how subversive a "slave of Christ" can be to the establishment (1 Cor 7:21–24). In the New Testament, all believers, whether Jew or Gentile, male or female, are "slaves of the Lord." It's a mark neither of sex nor of race, but of discipleship.

This is good news! But the biblical witness says even more than that. Mary's use of "God's slave" doesn't simply acknowledge God's call and her discipleship. It also places her in powerful Old Testament company. In taking this title, Mary self-consciously places herself among the great leaders of God's people. A psalmist speaks of Abraham as God's slave (105:42). Ezra the scribe and Malachi the prophet apply the designation to Moses (Neh 9:14; Mal 4:4). Moses' successor as the leader of Israel, Joshua, merits the title (Josh 24:29; Judg 2:8), as does Israel's greatest King, David (Ps 89:3). The Persian King,

Darius, speaks of the prophet Daniel as "the slave of the living God" (Dan 6:20). Even the Messiah will rule on David's throne as God's slave (Ezek 34:23).[7]

It's impossible to overstate just how impressive this group of men is. It includes the founding father, the deliverer, the military leader, the ruler and forefather of the Messiah, the faithful prophet in exile, and the embodiment of the nation's hope. All are defined by slavery to the Lord. In the biblical narrative, "God's slave" is anything but a title of weak-minded compliance. These men are God's chosen ones. Through them, God's plans for God's people come to pass.

And the Bible contains a small but elite list of women who fill similar leadership roles. In the story of the Exodus, readers meet Shiprah and Puah, who are remembered for the way they disobeyed Pharaoh's orders to kill all Israelite boys they helped deliver (Exod 1:15–22). Among the judges, few are as memorable as Deborah, a prophet and judge who led the less than courageous Barak and his army to victory over the forces of a Canaanite king named Jabin, and his general, Sisera. In the same story, another woman, Jael used sexually suggestive language to lure the fleeing Sisera into her tent, and having lulled him to sleep, killed him by driving a tent spike through his head (Judg 4–5). Judith, in the book that bears her name, rescued God's people from another general, Holofernes, by beheading him. Esther acted in a no less violent way to see that the Jews were saved from their enemies in Persia. When we compare Mary to these biblical women, the image of the compliant caregiver is utterly erased.[8]

Although the lists of both genders are striking, the women are especially so. In each case, God used small, insignificant characters—that they were female highlights their unimportance—to confound the designs of a much more powerful, male—again, gender plays a

---

7. Richard Bauckham, *Gospel Women* (Grand Rapids: Eerdmans, 2002), 66.
8. Ibid., 57, 66.

role here—enemy. These are the women whom Mary adopts as her company. They're the lenses through which we should read her story here. They're not weak! They're not in the Bible and in other ancient Jewish religious literature as examples of how women should behave in deference to men, or how slaves should behave in deference to masters. Rather, they're in the Bible as strong characters, speaking, acting, and leading on behalf of God in order that God's people may be liberated from their enemies.

"God's slave" is a daring, subversive, even counter-cultural title. If Mary is *God's* slave, chosen and constrained by God's will and plan, then she can be no one else's. If she's God's property, then she is not the property of her culture, her family, or her father. She doesn't even belong to her betrothed. Social mores and accepted practice—the "just the way things are" of everyday life—Mary freely, deliberately, and courageously sets aside through this speech. The absolute absence of Joseph from the annunciation story underscores this fact in a profound way. Gabriel announces, God calls, Mary assents, the Redeemer is conceived, and Joseph isn't even a witness to the events.

"God's slave" signals to us not only Mary's agreement to participate in the plan of God but also her understanding of God's authority in her life. It's a conscious adoption of lowly status to be sure, but it's the status of one who will be exalted by God. The Old Testament abounds with examples of such ironic reversals and Luke employs similar devices throughout his Gospel to great effect. So "God's slave" is a title that isn't uniquely Mary's as an individual, but it's a title uniquely hers as a representative of all followers of her Son, Jesus Christ.

Her concluding words underscore this fact: "May it be to me as you have spoken." Mary hasn't chosen this task for herself, any more than Saul had any choice when he was overwhelmed by his encounter with the Risen Lord on the road to Damascus (Acts 9:1–18). Like him, Mary's been chosen; like him, she freely assents to this choice. She will be God's slave, she will conceive in the midst of the social stigma that such a conception will create, she will bear a son, she will name him Jesus, she will embark on an uncertain future with a definitely inauspicious beginning because it's the unfolding of God's plan.

Some traditional interpretations of Mary see in these words a model for all women, whose ultimate calling is to bear and raise children. Feminist scholars have repeatedly pointed out that, because the child is conceived without intercourse, this ideal is absolutely unattainable and therefore harmful to Christian women. And they're right to do so. I would emphasize only that this objection is directed against a misreading of the Bible, rather than the Bible itself. If we attend to Mary's words of compliance and the biblical stories that provide their context, then it soon becomes clear that Luke's Mary isn't the model female (that is, the sex-free mother) but a model disciple (male or female) for the way she consents to what she doesn't yet fully understand. Mary has been chosen; Mary freely affirms God's choice. Mary has been granted divine favor and in her acceptance of that favor, she assumes the role of God's servant, God's slave. And to be a disciple with Mary is to live there, with her, hearing the liberating word of God as it calls us, constrains us, and ultimately frees us.

Truman and Mary ask the same question, but ultimately offer very different answers. Where is true human freedom found? For Truman, God's control and humanity's freedom inevitably come into conflict so that, for one to be true the other must be an illusion. And Truman makes no bones about the decision and its consequences. He wishes to be free; he must therefore leave Christof and the security and comfort he offers behind forever as he launches out into an off-screen unknown. God, in this view, is like a security blanket that we've knit but must put aside if we're to become true men and women. Mature. Free.

Mary, on the other hand, doesn't solve the mystery of human freedom and divine control for us. She doesn't give Truman's opposite answer—that we're really puppets, better off once we recognize it. If those were indeed the only alternatives, then we're better off with Truman, not with Mary. But that's not Mary's answer. She freely lives in response to the irresistible call. By accepting her role as

God's slave, she becomes a powerful leader of God's people. Her words indicate both that God is in control and that she is free. Her words present divine control and human freedom side by side in a beautiful symmetry.

To be a disciple with Mary is to recognize that Christ's disciples must both work out their salvation with fear and trembling and acknowledge that this very work—the work of mortifying and vivifying, the work of living and dying with Christ—is none other than the work of God in them (Phil 2:12–13). In so doing, God's word opens us to new dimensions of the Spirit, to new gifts, to new callings, to new roles that we couldn't have anticipated. To true freedom.

> Almighty God,
> you have created us to serve you,
> and in serving you, to be truly free.
> Grant that we with Mary will find
> our true freedom in your service,
> and in so doing become co-workers with your Son.
> For it is in His name
> that we pray.
> Amen.

For Reflection and Discussion

1. Watch *The Truman Show*. Do you sympathize with Truman? Why or why not? Compare Truman's conversation with Christof and Mary's with Gabriel. Which model of freedom—Truman or Mary—do you find more convincing or attractive? Why?

2. The title "God's slave" places Mary in some pretty violent company. Read over the stories of Deborah and Jael, Shiprah and Puah, Esther and Judith (if her book is in your Bible). Does Mary's deliberate association with these women inspire or unsettle you? Why?

3. Mary's acceptance of slavery is unique neither to her sex, nor her virginity, but to her role as a disciple. It transcends both her gender and her history to apply to all disciples. In what ways might such a commitment to God's service affect the day-to-day realities of your life?

4. The German reformer Martin Luther has written that the Christian is both bound to no one and the servant of all at the same time. In what ways might the story of the annunciation help to shed light on this statement?

5. Discipleship—as Lent reminds us—is hard work. Not only that, but it is also *our* work *and God's* work in us. For you, is the Bible's dual emphasis on human freedom and responsibility and divine control and activity comforting? Confusing? Frustrating? Think about ways these ideas will affect you this Lent.

She Who Believed
The Mystery of Faith

LUKE 1:39–45

"And blessed is she who has believed:
for there shall be a performance of those things
which were told her from the Lord."
(Luke 1:45, KJV)

We pick up Luke's story after the two annunciations contrasted in chapters one and two. As the story unfolds (Luke 1:39–45), Mary defies social convention again. This time, she leaves the house without a male escort to investigate the sign given by Gabriel. She hurries to Elizabeth's home in the Judean hill-country, presumably to see whether her much older cousin really is pregnant.

Of course, Mary's willingness to defy convention to serve God doesn't mean she had bad manners. When Mary enters Elizabeth's home, she follows the dictates of custom. She initiates the greeting with Elizabeth in deference and respect—because of Elizabeth's age and perhaps also because of her social status as the spouse of a priest, Elizabeth is Mary's better. Mary is observing the proper etiquette of the time.

But why would Luke, who's been perfectly happy to present Mary as willing to defy social custom, make a point of describing Mary's good manners and deference? To Luke's first readers, Mary's greeting of Elizabeth is simply what's expected—what younger, socially inferior people do. But Luke, fine author that he is, never wastes a word, let alone an entire scene. This greeting isn't just filler, a necessary device to move the story from one scene to the next. Rather, it serves the theme of the larger story. Luke has designed it to set the scene for a dramatic reversal that now begins to unfold.

No sooner has Mary completed her social obligations than the infant John leaps in Elizabeth's womb. Then Elizabeth herself is filled with the Holy Spirit. Under the Spirit's inspiration she prophetically proclaims that the younger, unmarried, ordinary Mary, in fact, surpasses her in every way! These are her words:

> "Blessed are you among women, and blessed is the fruit of your womb. And why has this happened to me, that the mother of my Lord comes to me? For as soon as I heard the sound of your greeting, the child in my womb leaped for joy. And blessed is she who believed that there would be a fulfillment of what was spoken to her by the Lord." (Luke 1:42b–45, NRSV)

Until this instant, Luke has been leading his readers to regard Elizabeth as Mary's better in every way: older, socially advanced, standing in the great biblical tradition of barren mothers. But with these words, Elizabeth snatches away our certainty and defies social custom yet again. Her young, single, pregnant cousin is "the mother of my Lord." Her visit is an unannounced, unanticipated gift of grace. She, not Elizabeth, is the Blessed One.

So while it may be easy for modern readers to pass over the contents of the paragraph, once we're sensitive to the context we become aware that to do so would be a huge mistake. Without background information, this paragraph seems simply to move readers from a larger narrative of angelic annunciation to a major poetic section, containing the songs of praise of Mary and Zechariah. Because it's both small and sandwiched between the sheer wonder of the angelic encounters and the theological depth of the songs, it's easily hidden. Even careful readers might miss its significance.

To overlook it, however, would be a terrible a loss, especially for those readers searching the Scriptures for guidance during Lent! This conversation between Elizabeth and Mary contains five fascinating details that disciples should consider seriously.

Note first Luke's emphasis on speech, not on any significant action. Mary simply hurries, enters, and greets—and that's about it. Speech moves the story forward. To now, we've witnessed the most extraordinary of events. The messenger of God, the angel Gabriel, has interrupted the lives of Zechariah, Elizabeth, and Mary, announcing to them that God has intervened in their lives in miraculous ways to advance his plans. Zechariah reacted with unbelief, Elizabeth with joy, Mary with acceptance. Now, in Elizabeth's prophetic utterance, we see just how much their lives have been changed by God's grace. Social conventions simply no longer apply when fidelity to God's word is at stake.

Second, in a brilliant narrative move, Luke has shrouded Mary's actual conception in absolute secrecy. Luke informs us with utmost delicacy that Elizabeth conceived after Zechariah returned home (Luke 1:23–24) and leaves us to surmise that the conception occurred in the usual way. Nothing, however, is said about Mary. After Gabriel delivers his message and departs, the scene switches to Mary's journey to the hill country. There is no indication of a miracle. That changes when Elizabeth begins her Spirit-inspired speech. Without being told, she knows what we readers have just found out: Mary has been specially chosen by God to bear a child who Elizabeth names as her Lord. Indeed, she knows more than we do. The conception— never narrated in Luke—has already occurred.

What was a future event just a few verses ago is now past. When the cousins meet, Mary is already pregnant. Luke thus shrouds Mary's conception in absolute mystery. He gives no alternate explanation. Just as no observers were present at the miracle of creation, none are present at the miracle of the conception of Jesus, an event defying explanation. Elizabeth can't explain it, but can only bear witness to it. This remarkable silence, I think, drives us back to the words of Gabriel: "Nothing is impossible with God." Mary has seen the sign. Mary has heard the word. Mary and we now know for certain that what God has promised has already begun to come to pass.

Third, notice that Elizabeth calls Mary the mother of "my Lord." This is significant. The Greek word is *Kyrios* and can mean simply, "sir," or more strongly, "master." But attentive readers will note that Luke employs the word Lord extensively in chapter 1—seven times, in fact, and always as a title for God. Elizabeth and Zechariah, Luke says, observe the Lord's commandments (v. 6); Zechariah served in the Lord's temple (v. 9); the angel of the Lord appeared to him (v. 11); Zechariah's son will be great in the Lord's sight (v. 15); he will lead many back to the Lord their God (v. 16); he will prepare a people for the Lord (v. 17); Elizabeth recognizes her pregnancy is a miracle of the Lord (v. 25). Clearly, at least in this chapter, "Lord" has a focused meaning—it's a synonym for God. And God, Elizabeth knows, is an unborn child in the womb of a Palestinian teenager. Elizabeth knows this because her own baby leaped for joy at the sound of Mary's voice.

This leads us to our fourth observation. We usually think of the ministry of John the Baptizer as beginning with his appearance in the wilderness, in Luke chapter 3. Right here, filled with the Holy Spirit in utero, the infant John is already going on ahead of the Lord, preparing the Lord's people for his coming. It's not that the infant John, still in his mother's womb, already possesses some kind of advanced awareness, enabling him to know what's going on around him and consciously reacting to it. But the Holy Spirit, who has prophetically gifted John, is even now at work. The Holy Spirit has so called John to prepare the way of the Lord that John, even unaware and in the womb, begins to fulfill that calling.

Fifth, notice that Elizabeth blesses Mary twice: she's about to become the mother of the Lord (Luke 1:42) and she believed that what God had promised would come to pass (Luke 1:45). When Elizabeth first blesses Mary and her unborn child, the word Luke uses is *eulogoumene*, from which the English word eulogy derives; it means roughly, "commended" or perhaps even more strongly, "adored." The emphasis falls on Mary's place in the human family—granted to her because of the son she bears, it's still a place of exaltation. Because of Jesus, says Elizabeth, Mary will forever be commended, adored, or blessed by her fellow human beings.

What English readers may well miss in the second blessing is a very important change in wording. This time Elizabeth says that Mary is *makaria*. The word can mean "happy" but that misses the depth of the biblical tradition that uses the word to mean "favored by God." This is especially the case in the Greek translation of certain Psalms, with which a Greek-speaking Christian like Luke would have been most familiar. Here the emphasis falls on Mary's place in God's plan. She is uniquely favored by God and this favor will be made evident as the announcement made by Gabriel actually comes to pass.

Recognizing the change in vocabulary, and the switch in focus from human adoration to divine generosity, not only adds needed nuance to our English translations, but also helps readers avoid a potentially serious misreading of Elizabeth's words. If we miss their emphasis on the graciousness and favor of God made plain in the fulfillment of God's promise, the words seem to indicate that the source of Mary's blessing is not God, but her belief. On this misunderstanding of the text, it is as a consequence of her belief that God would do what he promised through Gabriel, that Mary stands in a favored relationship with God. Speaking strictly in terms of the grammar of the original language, this reading is possible. But it is not right.

The change in vocabulary from *eulegomene* to *makaria* reminds readers of what has been a central theme of Luke's all along: the radical and free nature of God's grace. God's favor on Mary, which up til now has been known only in secret and only as a result of divine intervention, will be soon publicly seen because what God has promised to Mary will come to pass in a most public way. She has become pregnant and will in due time give birth. There's probably no experience more intensely emotional and intensely obvious for a woman. And everyone who sees Mary and her child will see the fulfillment of the promise. That—not Mary's act of belief—is the blessing.

In Elizabeth's eyes, Mary is doubly favored: she's adored by her fellow human beings because of the child she bears; her pregnancy and motherhood is proof of God's favor. Mary is blessed not because of some inner quality, some special pious capacity that is uniquely hers, some virtue the rest of us lack. She's blessed because of her child and because of God's dramatic action. She's blessed as she points away from herself and to her son, Jesus. We have already reflected on Mary as the object of God's gracious choice, and there's a similar theme here. The source of Mary's blessedness—both in terms of her status in the human family and her status with God—is not her, but her son, himself the fulfillment of God's promise, who is none other than the Lord come among his people.

But at the same time, in these same passages of Scripture, Luke refuses to paint Mary as a passive recipient of divine goodwill. He doesn't allow readers to see Mary as a character to whom things happen, but who remains fundamentally out of control of her life. Set against God's gracious choice and the certain fulfillment of God's miraculous promise is Mary saying, "Here am I, the servant of the Lord," and Elizabeth saying, "Blessed is she that believed." Short sentences to be sure, but they reveal a subtler picture. To be sure, Mary's blessedness derives from God's promise and its sure fulfillment, but Mary chooses this destiny as her own. "Blessed is she who believed." Mary's pilgrimage of faith begins in simple trust in the grace of God.

Luke's portrayal of Mary throughout this first chapter, and especially here, in the prophetic announcement of Elizabeth, is reminiscent of the Old Testament stories of Abraham, Moses, Samuel, and Isaiah. In each case, God called and commissioned his chosen ones for a special purpose, whether it was to be the father of a people, or their deliverer, judge, or prophet.

And for each of those Old Testament characters, the call elicited a response of trust. In trust, Abraham left his home and his extended family to become a nomad in search of a country that would be given not so much to him, as to his descendants. In trust, Moses went with Aaron to Egypt to speak God's word of liberation not only to the enslaved Israelites, but also to the enslaving Pharaoh. In trust, he took the people to the edge of the land promised to Abraham but was forbidden to enter it himself. In trust, Samuel responded to a voice calling in the night, commissioning him to be a prophet and a judge in Israel. In trust, Samuel was faithful to that vocation even though in so doing, he diminished his own political power. In trust, Isaiah declared his willingness to be God's mouthpiece to God's people. And in trust, he fulfilled that role even though the message he delivered was unpopular, unaccepted, and culminated in his own death.

When we read Mary's response through the lenses of these biblical stories, we find that it has nothing to do with what is commonly understood by words like passivity and servility. Mary doesn't submit to coercion—she freely consents to the working of God's grace in and through her. Mary makes an active, conscious, free and faith-filled choice to participate in God's destiny for her. Mary chooses God's choice of her. Mary exemplifies Christian faith and discipleship in her trustful hearing of the word of God and in her free and glad consent to the gracious choice of God. As a result, like Abraham, Moses, Samuel and Isaiah, Mary is numbered among the great leaders of God's people. Elizabeth is right to say of her, "Blessed is she that believed."

Before we move from the first century to the twenty-first, let's draw three conclusions about this part of Luke's story. First, adoration of Mary is a right and proper attitude for believers to cultivate. Luke hastens to add, however, that Mary is to be adored not for herself, her virtues, or her own inherent goodness. We don't adore her because she was able to convince God of her worthiness to bear God's Son. Rather, we adore her because God in grace chose her to be the mother of the Lord; because she herself is the vehicle through which God would enter the world. To be sure, the incarnation of God in Mary's womb was an intervention eternal in scope and purpose, part of God's plan. But it was also a plan enacted in this limited, dependent, world *through her*. We may rightly say, therefore, not only with Elizabeth but also with those millions of Christians who have made the Hail Mary an expression of their own piety: "Blessed are you among women and blessed is the fruit of your womb."

This human adoration is rooted in the divine favor. We adore Mary because she stands in a unique relationship to God. As a daughter of the people of Israel, she has already been chosen to be a light to the Gentiles. But the choice is even more specific, for out of all the women in Israel who shared in that general calling, she was singled out to be the mother of the Lord. She is therefore doubly blessed. She is to be adored by us because she is especially favored by God. We fail to do justice to Luke's Gospel when we shy away from saying so.

Finally, though Mary's trust in God's gracious intervention in her life didn't provide the basis for God's blessing, it remains exemplary for all disciples of her Son. Mary freely and gladly consented to God's electing grace without knowing just what she was agreeing to. Her confidence doesn't lie in certainty about the future, but in the identity of the one who knows the future because he has planned it. The God of Israel, Mary well knew, was one who made promises and kept them. She is blessed not because of some inherent ability to predict the outcome, but because the outcome is secured by the reliability of the One who made the promise. Mary is a model of what it means to trust completely in God, a model of confident reliance. As she who believed, she stands before us today, her example inviting us to a similar confident commitment.

How can this remarkable woman shape our Christian journeys this Lent? Let's look at what we've already discovered. First, God's grace frees us from both despair and pride as we face the difficult work of growing in holiness. Second, God's grace is the ground of our freedom; apart from it, we're enslaved to our own sinful desires and destructive habits. For us as much as for Mary, God's grace elicits a response of trust. What does such trust look like for us?

The answer is different for everyone. But we can draw three general guidelines from Luke that we ought always to keep in mind. First, if Mary's life before the angelic announcement is any indication, it's not trust based on present personal circumstances. Mary doesn't entrust her body and her future to God on the basis of how God had dealt with her already—after all, her living conditions weren't exactly signs of God's blessing.

Luke's Gospel contains no back-story that explains why Mary trusted God, why she freely embraced her destiny as the twice-blessed mother of the Lord. So let's dig a little deeper. Mary isn't old or devout like Elizabeth and Zechariah—she's absolutely and utterly ordinary. On all the details that have for generations fired the imaginations of the curious and devout, Luke is silent.

This combination of biblical silence and pious interest has led Christians over the centuries to fill in Luke's gap, creating a story to explain why Mary acted the way she did. The most popular attempt is a document written in the middle of the second century called the *Proto-Gospel of James*. Its anonymous writer uses a literary device that still pops up from time to time in contemporary historical novels, adopting the character of a witness to the events in the gospel. The character, or persona, is that of James, the half-brother of the Lord, and the gospel is one of many ancient Christian fictional works that appealed to pious fascination with the childhoods of Jesus and Mary. It proved to be so popular that it was once accepted as Holy Scripture by some theologians of the Eastern Church. Others in the West—especially Jerome—rightly called it a baseless legend. Either way, there's no denying the influence this document has had on succeeding generations of Christians.

The *Proto-Gospel of James* describes the piety and relative wealth of Mary's parents, Joachim and Anna, and in fact, gives us their names. It portrays Mary's conception much like that of John the Baptist's: as a miraculous compensation for her parents' age. It describes her childhood as one of rarefied purity, with much of it spent living in the temple and eating food provided by an angel. It accounts her betrothal at the age of twelve to an aged Joseph, a relationship more akin to a guardianship than a marriage intended to preserve her virginity. What an unreal childhood! The entire document is so concerned, in fact, to accent Mary's purity that it completely removes Mary from the world the rest of us live in. As a result, this Mary isn't surprised at all by the Annunciation. But a Mary who isn't surprised by Gabriel's visit and announcement isn't Luke's Mary at all.

And that's a problem. Popular stories like this one move us away from Luke's text, distracting us from the literary and theological points he's making— especially that Mary, by conventional standards, is a most unlikely candidate for God's blessing. We've already seen how Luke contrasts Mary with Zechariah and Elizabeth—against the pious, priestly couple, Mary seems ordinary in every way. Indeed, if any of the three should have trusted in God on the basis of previous blessings, it was the priest, Zechariah. And he doubted! This is underscored by the deference that Mary shows to Elizabeth in this short paragraph. As far as she knows, social customs are still in place and there was no reason to treat Elizabeth as anything other than her social better.

Luke's Mary isn't terribly pious, and her social position isn't impressive. So let's imagine Mary as just like other first century Palestinian teenage girls. She's probably around fourteen—just entering the age of marriageability. But she looks much older than her years— her skin has been toughened by desert sand and sun. She understands herself to be the property of her father, and soon to be the property of her husband and her role in life is to have children. She cannot read. Her piety, such as it is, is grounded not in holy texts, but in holy stories she's heard from infancy. This, and not some rarified temple-dwelling beauty, is the teenager baffled by the strange events in which she's caught up. Luke's Mary doesn't trust based on her past.

Second, Mary's response of trust isn't based on any future guarantees. The last time we meet Mary in the Bible, she's in the upper room waiting for the coming of the Holy Spirit and the beginning of the mission of the Church to take the gospel of the Lord Jesus to the nations. After that, nothing. The Bible speaks not one word about Mary's later life, including how—or even whether—she died. But Christian tradition is filled with stories, beginning in the East and spreading through the Christian world, that seek to fill in this gap.

One Roman Catholic nun, Sister Mary of Agreda, relates a series of visions in which she's granted details of Mary's later life. Preserved in her four-volume (!) book entitled *The Mystical City of God* Sister Mary insists that at the resurrection of Christ, Mary was taken into heaven. From there, she was sent back to earth where she enjoyed a career as a teacher of the apostles, a powerful exorcist, and miracle-working missionary. And at the end of this stellar course of earthly life, Mary was taken body and soul into heaven where she now reigns.

I don't mean to poke fun at people who believe stories like these but to point out that wherever these details come from, they don't come from the Bible. Some of them may well be true—the bodily assumption of Mary into heaven is, after all, a dogma of the Roman Catholic Church.

The angel Gabriel does indeed speak of the future in his announcement to Mary. But that future has nothing to do with her. That future has to do with her son. "He will be great. He will be called the Son of the Most High. He will reign on David's throne forever." This is all well and good, but it's not the sound of a bargain being struck. Gabriel doesn't convey God's promise as an exchange: "your trust, Mary, for my reward." Mary is promised no reward at all, no guarantee that her future would share in the glory of her son's, no insight into how that glory would be worked out. There's no promise of future safety and wealth and no guarantee of a lifetime of health and happiness to which Mary could appeal as a basis for her trust in God.

Third, if confidence can't be found in her past or future, what then is the basis for Mary's trust? Is it a blind leap into the dark that Elizabeth commends and we are to emulate? No. Mary's trust does have a foundation. And it's that foundation that makes it commendable and exemplary. For Mary's trust is based solely on the character of the One who promised. Mary's trust is grounded in the reliability of God, whom she would have learned from childhood, is not like human beings who lie and change their minds. The God of Abraham, Isaac, and Jacob is a God who makes promises and keeps them. That's what Mary knew. That's why she believed the word of the angel and embraced a destiny that changed her life, the corporate life of her people, and the collective life of the human race.

And Luke takes great pains to convince his readers that they stand in similar situations, facing similar invitations. That's why there are so many Old Testament allusions in these first two chapters. Luke uses these allusions literarily and theologically to anchor Mary's story in the history of God's dealings with his people (what some theologians call salvation-history). But there's a pastoral purpose too. If Luke's Mary is a model disciple—and I think she is—if we are to strive to make her story our own, then we should consider our own stories in the light not only of hers, but also in the light of all the other biblical stories that lurk in Luke's writings.

Stories of the great matriarchs and patriarchs of Israel; stories of political leaders and prophets. Stories of men and women specially chosen by God. These, says Luke, are not only the back-story for Mary but the back-story of all those who have in baptism entrusted themselves to Mary's Son. In Mary and in the stories scattered throughout Luke's account of her amazing actions, we have a description of God's character. And through his account of this first disciple, Luke invites his readers to trust in God and in God's promise also.

But isn't this supposed to be a book about Lent? A book about becoming holy? About unlearning bad habits and learning new ones and engaging in active discipleship? After all, discipleship is focused on doing things. So shouldn't this book be about discipleship improvement techniques—praying more and more effectively, fasting without feeling too hungry, cultivating a spirit of generosity, repenting, being less worldly and more godly? But this isn't a book about spiritual techniques—though there's not necessarily anything wrong with them.

Instead, now half way through the book, you have read only about God. About God's grace; about how that grace liberates us for service; about how grace invites a response of confident trust in the God who makes and keeps promises. But perhaps this is the most important Lenten lesson of all: Christian discipleship begins and ends in grace. All our efforts, all our spiritual exercises and devotional disciplines—and these are important—are grounded in, are made possible by, are responses to the radical, free, favor of God that comes before all our works.

God loves you. He invites you to trust, offering no pointers from your past and no guarantees about the future. God invites you only to consider God's character. His reliability. His ability to do what he said. His unending faithfulness. Will you be blessed with Mary? Will you place your trust in God?

Faithful God,
you have visited us with your grace
and have invited us to trust in your promise.

May we like Mary,
find our confidence only in your character
and entrust ourselves wholly to your care.
This we pray
in Jesus' name,
Amen.

For Reflection and Discussion

1. Elizabeth's blessing of Mary is twofold—she's to be both adored and commended. In your own life, in what ways might Mary be adored?

2. Mary trusted in God's promise based on her understanding of God's character. Imagine yourself in her situation. In your opinion, is this really any more than a leap in the dark? Does it really merit Elizabeth's prophetic praise? Think about ways you've trusted in God's character. What was the experience like in your life?

3. So far, Luke has alluded to many other biblical tales. In what ways do the stories of Abraham (Gen 12:1–9), Moses (Exod 3:1–22), Samuel (1 Sam 3:1–4:1), and Isaiah (Isa 6:1–13) add to or influence your understanding of Mary's story? How do they fit with the other Old Testament stories already considered?

4. Luke invites his readers to see their own stories as continuous with those of the Old Testament and that of Mary herself. How does your perception of your own story change as you read it "within" the larger, biblical one?

5. Does the emphasis on grace we've talked about detract from Lent's traditional focus on discipline and growth in holiness? Why?

6. In what ways does our culture keep us from forming trusting relationships not only with God, but with other people? What advice do you believe Luke would offer to people in these kinds of situations?

Filled with Good Things
The Mystery of Poverty

LUKE 1: 46–56

"He hath put down the mighty from their seats,
and exalted them of low degree.
He hath filled the hungry with good things;
and the rich he hath sent empty away."

(Luke 1:53, KJV)

Life ought to be fair. Absolutely and utterly fair. It's a moral truism drilled into us in church sanctuaries, in family living rooms, on the playing field, and even in the classroom, where I experience the platitude's force regularly. Lack of fairness is one of the most common complaints I run into as a college teacher. "But Dr. Perry, it's not fair!" has been the response to grades (which would have been higher, had I been fair), assignments (which would have been either easier or fewer or both, again, had I been fair), even class meeting times (my classes would have been scheduled differently, had I been fair). I've never quite figured out how fairness figures in these situations—especially scheduling, which I have no control over whatsoever. But there's no denying that few things upset undergraduates more than the perception that they or their friends have been treated unfairly.

Of course, "life ought to be fair" is far more than a pop-culture ethical absolute. In the past, it was also the backbone of one of the most influential arguments for the existence of God in Western philosophy. Immanuel Kant insisted on a universal human awareness of right and wrong that made sense only in a universe that had been created by a moral God who would reward virtue and punish vice with unquestionable equanimity. In other words, based on his understanding of human morality, Kant insisted that life ought to be fair and God had to exist in order to guarantee that it would be. Whether Kant's argument is a good one is a question that we can leave to philosophers. What I find interesting is that perhaps the most influential Western philosopher (whether we're familiar with his name or not) after Saint Thomas Aquinas insisted that God would, whether in this life or in the next, see that each got what he or she deserved. That God would be, above everything else, fair.

But is Kant's god—this fair god—well, God? Is the god who treats all people equally according to blind justice the God of the Bible? "Blind justice" is a deliberately chosen metaphor. For when we speak about "blind justice," we're in fact not talking about the God and Father of the Lord Jesus. Whether we know it or not, we're actually talking about the ancient Roman goddess Justitia. If you're, like me, a fan of Dick Wolf's long-running TV series *Law and Order*, you should know Justitia well. For you see her almost once per episode. She is the blindfolded woman holding both scales and a sword whose statue stands either outside or inside any number of courthouses.

It's worth remembering that Justitia has a history that's both religious and non-Christian. That many of us simply don't realize that when we see her shows just how widespread her image and her ideal have become. Not even members of the ACLU blink when they see her. Of course, erecting statues of Justitia at courthouses is not state establishment of religion. And to enter that discussion is to miss my point: before we can talk about God being fair, we need first to be willing to ask ourselves just what deity we're talking about.

If we're talking about a God who's fair, then we're not talking about the God of the Bible. Just? Absolutely. God is just. But the Bible doesn't define justice (whether human or divine) as fairness. We don't have to look any further than the first three Lenten lessons in this book for examples. These chapters describe a deity who is manifestly unfair, a God who doesn't reward according to our behavior, but according to mercy and grace.

Luke has described for us a God who is merciful—a God who withholds punishment. He has described a God who is gracious—a God who actually blesses people regardless of their morality, spirituality, or status. A God who is gracious and merciful, who is slow to anger and abounding in faithful love: that's Luke's God. And it's Luke's God because it's the God of the Old Testament and the God of Jesus and the God of the first Christians. And that God, precisely because of these wonderful attributes, is just but not fair.

When we talk about the justice of the Christian God, talk of fairness has to stop. In the passage we'll look at now, Luke adds a new wrinkle: this God that Christians worship is not only unfair because he's gracious and merciful, but also because he actively takes sides. God isn't a referee in human conflicts. God is a player! God is actively involved. In the passage that we are about to think about, Luke and Mary will tell us that God has chosen the side of the powerless, the marginalized, and the oppressed, and taken sides against the powerful, the wealthy, and the oppressors. God will exalt those whom this world regards as insignificant. God will save the world through them.

We've already seen this theme written between the lines. Now it's loud and clear in Mary's only extended speech in the entire Bible:

And Mary said,
"My soul magnifies the Lord,
    and my spirit rejoiced in God my Savior,
for he had looked with favor on the
    lowliness of his servant.

Surely, from now on all generations
     will call me blessed;
for the Mighty One has done great
     things for me,
     and holy is his name.
His mercy is for those who fear him
     from generation to generation.

He has shown strength with his arm;
     he has scattered the proud in the thoughts of their hearts.
He has brought down the powerful
     from their thrones,
     and lifted up the lowly;
he has filled the hungry with good things,
     and sent the rich away empty.

He has helped his servant Israel,
     in remembrance of his mercy,
according to the promise he made to our ancestors,
     to Abraham and to his descendants forever."
     And Mary remained with her about three months and then
          returned to her home. (Luke 1:46–56)

This is one of the most beautiful passages of the New Testament. It's sometimes called the Magnificat (from its first word in Latin translation) or Mary's song. It's prayed or sung regularly as part of the liturgy of several Christian traditions.

It's also Mary's only lengthy speech in either Luke's Gospel or the New Testament. Up till now, her words have been minimal: she's questioned the angel, accepted the Lord's call, and greeted Elizabeth. Now she sings a sustained song of praise to God that accomplishes two important tasks in the story. It gives us Mary's interpretation of the strange and wondrous sequence of events into which she's been pulled. And it gives us Luke's interpretation of Mary's role in his Gospel as a whole.

Mary's song seems to fall into four segments: an introduction (1:46b–47), two verses (1:48–50 and 51–53), and a conclusion (1: 54–55). Let's look briefly at each one. In the introduction, words strongly reminiscent not only of Hannah (1 Sam 2:1–3) but also the Psalms (Ps 35:9) and the prophet Habakkuk (Hab 3:18) offer praise to the God of Mary's salvation. In fact, scholars have documented the deep infusion of the entire song with the themes and words of the Old Testament. In the light of their literary work, it's no exaggeration to say that the Magnificat is a summary of the entire Old Testament.

Through these allusions, Luke has again gone to great lengths to present Mary as part of a larger story. God may indeed be doing something new for the salvation of the world through her, but God isn't acting without precedent. The Old Testament story of God is the story of One who grants the heartfelt prayers of barren mothers like Hannah, who inspires the praises of psalmists and prophets by rescuing them from calamity. And this God is acting again.

When Mary is inspired to proclaim that God's intervention is gracious and merciful, for the weak at the expense of the strong, she's become a prophet, declaring God's intentions behind the events that have just taken place. And her prophetic linkage between God's salvation and the conception of Jesus in her womb exalts Mary further—she alone is the vehicle through which God's entrance into human history, what theologians call the Incarnation, will take place.

This exaltation is elaborated in the first of the two verses. While each verse gives the motivations for the praise that springs from Mary's soul, they do so in different ways. The first paints a picture of God as the Mighty Warrior who fights on behalf of his chosen ones and against their enemies. This God remembers those who fear him. This God lavishes his mercy on those who call upon God's name. This is the God who has intervened in Mary's life. This is not a picture of a judge presiding over a legal proceeding without getting his hands dirty. This is a picture of a God up to his elbows in human misery, fighting to rescue people from certain death.

We're meant to understand that Mary's exaltation isn't doled out by a strictly just God as a reward for some previously unknown, in-built capacity for righteousness or piety. Rather, Mary declares her position to be lowly. She claims again her role as the Lord's slave. And we're meant to conclude that God has taken her side. God has embraced her cause. God has become her champion. It's God's unanticipated favor that's brought Mary from lowliness to greatness. Because of God's intervention she'll be the mother of him whose kingdom will have no end (Luke 1:33), who will establish God's mercy from generation to generation.

This enables Mary then to predict that Elizabeth's twofold blessing will extend beyond Elizabeth's own words to become a universal acknowledgement of Mary's singular position before God. Because of God's intervention, Mary adds that Elizabeth's double blessing, which we talked about above, will eventually move beyond Elizabeth's home, beyond Roman occupied Palestine, beyond the Jewish race, even beyond the first century. All generations, she says, will declare the favor God has lavished on her, his servant.

The second verse moves from a picture of God who works actively for those who fear him to a picture of God who works actively against those who trust in their own strength. When God takes the side of those who fear him and takes up the cause of the poor and the oppressed, then the designs of the proud, the mighty, and the rich are frustrated while the lowly are raised and the hungry are filled with good things.

Some biblical literary critics have made the interesting suggestion that the past tense of the verbs in this section (brought, lifted, filled, and sent) shows that Luke has taken a hymn about what God has done through the death and resurrection of Jesus and placed it on Mary's lips. If Luke did so—I think the argument is persuasive—he makes a strong claim about the saving significance of the whole of Jesus' life from the instant of his conception. For him, God's intervention on behalf of the poor and oppressed isn't to be limited to God's act in the cross and resurrection (though it's certainly there, too). God has displayed strength not by inspiring armies, or calling people to arms. God has confounded the powerful through the miraculous conception of a baby. This baby will confound the plans of the powerful. This baby will forever transform the fortunes of the lowly.

There's no greater image of bias possible. The lowly will triumph over the exalted. The poor will be fed and rich sent away hungry because God has taken sides, in a way that fully embraces the lot of the weakest of the weak. He does so as a human infant. Because God has taken sides, a fetus will frustrate the plans of kings!

Finally, in the conclusion, Mary ties both verses to the fulfillment of God's promise to Abraham and his descendents. God isn't simply the Mighty Warrior; God is also the great Promise Keeper. The conception of Jesus, in other words, is how God's promises made to Abraham, Isaac, Jacob and their descendants will finally come to pass. This is the climax both of the way Mary understands herself and the way Luke understands Mary's place in God's plan. Mary is the embodiment of the people of Israel, the one in whom Israel's calling to be a light to the Gentiles will be specifically fulfilled. God has remembered his covenant promise this way: he has both frustrated the plans of the powerful and raised the lowly and the poor. This is the story of the Old Testament. Now, the pinnacle of such divine action is the miraculous conception of the Son of God in the womb of the Virgin. It's the greatest reversal of all. This is the message of Mary, the prophet.

The question to ask now: what does Mary the prophet and her message of God's unfair justice have to do with us? This is where the themes of Lent come to the fore. If Lent is about mortification, and allowing the gospel to expose the habits and attitudes and dispositions that need to be judged and destroyed by God, then we should pay close attention to what Mary says about God's justice and about those who receive it. If Lent is about vivification, about allowing the gospel to create and nurture and develop those habits and attitudes and dispositions that bring our perspective on the world into line with God's, then we should pay close attention to what Mary says about God's justice and those who receive it. As we take our Lenten journey with Mary, let's think about these responses to Mary's song.

First, Mary's song of praise about this just and unfair God ought to discipline our own sense of what justice is. While our culture engrains in us the notion that justice means that everyone gets what they deserve— no more and no less—God's justice is all about actively taking sides in favor of those who have no visible means of support. Enacting that kind of justice, of course, doesn't force us into supporting this or that or the other political party (in Canada, where I live, there are five national parties, four of which have cross-country support). Christians should, it seems to me, be especially wary of their language being co-opted by political parties of whatever ideological stripe—and besides, this isn't what I mean by enacting God's justice. (More on that later.)

Second, as Mary's song disciplines our sense of justice, bringing it into line with God's, it just might call us to question our allegiances. It ought to invite us to ask whether, in our jobs, personal relationships, retirement savings plans, we've identified ourselves with those whom Mary calls the proud, the powerful, and the rich.

Mary's song isn't a blanket condemnation of wealth. Her target is very specific, and the prophets of the Old Testament (especially Amos) aim at it all the time. The people Mary names are those who, in the eyes of the prophets, get their wealth at the expense of the poor, who maintain their wealth by exploiting the poor, and who hoard it rather than share it with the poor. They're the ones who treat wealth as a zero-sum game, determined to be the winners. They're the ones Mary names as God's enemies. In the end, they'll be sent away humiliated, empty and hungry. Mary invites everyone who's serious about Lent's insistence on mortification to ask just whose side they're really on.

Third, as Mary's song disciplines our sense of justice, bringing it into line with God's, it will at some point compel us to side with those whom God has chosen. Again, Mary's very clear about who they are: the lowly and the hungry. Again, her language is rooted in the prophets of the Old Testament who cried out for justice on behalf of the widows, the orphans, and the aliens. Women without husbands; children without parents; people without family networks: in other words, people who fell through the cracks of the ancient Israelite social safety net. People, in other words, with no visible means of support.

In our culture, the labels we might use would be different: the homeless, the working poor, single parents. But the idea is the same. God's justice is actively on the side of those whom society forgets. We may not all be called to kiss the feet of a beggar, as Saint Francis of Assisi did; nor may we all be called to go to Calcutta to care for dying people as Mother Theresa did. Of course, these examples are as obvious as they are extreme. But there are other ways to see our justice come into line with God's.

A church in Winnipeg, Manitoba, where I live, enacts God's justice by buying abandoned houses from the city, repairing and renovating them, and selling them to working class families who probably would never be able to buy their own home otherwise. This creates jobs, creates neighborhoods and renews urban spaces, and gives people a sense of dignity and worth they might otherwise have never found. A perfect example of practical, simple actions with local, tangible results. A perfect example of God's justice at work. I have no idea what might work in your community. But you do. And Lent is a good time to think about it.

Just God
You have entered our history
through the Virgin's womb, on the side of the lowly.

May we, with her,
ally ourselves not with the proud and powerful
but stand on the side of the poor and powerless.

We ask humbly
in Jesus' name.
Amen.

For Reflection and Discussion

1. How do you think about everyday justice? How does Mary's song challenge or contradict or affirm the way you understand what justice is?

2. How does the image of Mary as a prophet seem to you? Curious? Comforting? Worrisome? Wrong? Why?

3. What do you think about the way Luke locates the victory of God over the powerful not in Jesus' cross, but in his conception?

4. Does the notion of God as a warrior who takes sides for some and against others encourage you? Anger you? Confuse you? Why?

5. As we bring our conception of justice into line with God's, we begin to question some of our allegiances (mortification) and begin to make new ones (vivification). How might this played out in your life? In the life of your church community?

6. Think about ways you and/or your church community can begin to enact the kind of justice that Mary describes. What practical steps can you undertake to see these take place?

Ponder These Things

The Mystery of the Future

LUKE 2:1–20, 41–52

But Mary kept all these things,
and pondered them in her heart.
(Luke 2:19, KJV)

And [Jesus] went down with them,
and came to Nazareth, and was subject unto them:
but his mother kept all these sayings in her heart
(Luke 2:51, KJV)

Let's look at two small sections of Luke's account of Jesus' birth and childhood. They're tied together by their vocabulary and by the way they each help the story move forward. At the end of each story, two phrases are repeated, and when knit together, they're important. Each story ends with a variation of "Mary kept all these things in her heart." What things does Mary keep in her heart? In what way? Why? These are important questions. Answering them will give us even more insight into Mary's nature and help enlighten our own discipleship journeys during Lent and beyond.

The first passage is Luke's version of the birth of Jesus. This story—with its shepherds, angels, and manger scene—is for many people (both Christian and not) *the* Christmas story. Through its annual repetition in churches and its representation in nativity scenes on lawns and holiday cards, this passage has become almost too familiar to us. But looking at it again, with eyes opened by the disciplines of Lent rather than clouded by the cultural celebration of Christmas, just might show us something new. So let's revisit the story in detail.

It falls into three parts. The first anchors our story in politics and history. In the days of Caesar Augustus, while Quirinius governed Syria, it begins; a census was decreed that required everyone to return to the town of their birth. Some modern commentators have noted that there might be a chronological error here. Whether there is or not—and there are just as many commentators who defend Luke's account—Luke is deliberately tying his story to real events. He wants his readers to know that what's about to happen in his story happens in the real world—not some mythical world of dying and rising gods, but the hard world of Roman Emperors. And our world, too. For our world—just as much as Luke's—isn't of our own making, but defined for us by those in power.

Having located his story in time and space, Luke reintroduces his characters. First on the scene is Joseph. Following the instructions of the occupying government, he leaves his home in Nazareth in the northern region of Galilee to return to Bethlehem in the south; as a descendent of David, Bethlehem was his ancestral family home.

Then comes Mary. What has she been doing until now? Luke doesn't say. In fact, after completing her wonderful, prophetic song of praise, Mary exits the stage and only returns now. In the interim, Luke has turned his and our attention to the birth and naming of John the Baptizer.

Now, as Mary returns to center stage, her miraculous pregnancy seems overwhelmed by the political affairs of everyday life. Caesar has decreed. Quirinius will administer. Joseph will obey. Mary may well be pregnant with the Messiah, the Son of God, but politics are politics and political life doesn't wait for anyone—not even God. Mary is powerless in relation to the political might of Rome. Almost as an afterthought, Luke tells us that Mary, Joseph's pregnant betrothed, has made the trip with him to Bethlehem, to the family homestead. To anyone who noticed Mary—and probably no one did— she would have looked like a typical first-century Palestinian woman. She'd have seemed weak and insignificant, as the men who ruled her life—from as far away as Rome and as close as home—made the decisions whose consequences she'd have to live with whether she wanted to or not.

Of course, by now we're used to Luke's strategy of challenging the accepted order of things. It may well have been the accepted order of things that women were passive, submissive, and obedient. But remember, when we're dealing with Mary, nothing is how it appears. We're not dealing with just anyone—we're dealing with God's slave, with someone whose significance surpasses the patriarchs, whose company is the great female liberators of God's people. Things may look like business as usual, but as always for Luke, there's so much more going on.

This strategy surfaces when Mary re-enters the scene. To those on the outside, this woman may well look like just another cog in the great Roman machine. But to believers in Jesus, this picture is inadequate. Once Mary is back on the scene, she's dynamic. Look at all the active verbs Luke uses in his narration: When the days of her pregnancy were fulfilled, she gave birth; she swaddled her first-born; she laid him in a manger.

The irony is both thick and delightful. On the one hand, Luke narrates Jesus' birth and Mary's actions as utterly trivial. In the shadow of the great Caesar's attempt to manipulate the whole world by not simply ordering a census, but ordering his global administrative structure to carry it out, what is the birth of a baby in a backwater province? What are the actions of that baby's mother? Why should we care?

On the other hand, we should care because—as Luke will make clear in the rest of his story—the birth of this baby signals the beginning of God's judgment and the beginning of the end of Caesar's reign. The world doesn't yet know it. It proceeds as though nothing important has happened (and, alas, this is still true). But Mary, the first Christians, and we know something different. We've heard the words of Gabriel. We've heard Mary's assent. We've heard the blessing of Elizabeth. We've heard the song of prophetic praise. And what we know now as prophetic insight will soon, in Luke's story, become public knowledge.

The second part of the story opens abruptly in verse 8. In a not so subtle shift of location, readers are taken from the stable in which the new-born Lord enters human history to the fields, to meet shepherds who are watching their flocks by night. It is to these shepherds—not to Caesar, not to the governor, not even to the inn-keeper or Joseph—that God sends his angelic army to announce the fulfillment of his promise, the birth of his Son. The *Gloria* announcing the birth of the Savior of the world comes not to the halls of power, not to the centers of commerce, but to the margins, the outskirts of civilized life—to men whose role in the society of the day was both necessary and suspect.

The shepherds, understandably, are terrified. Dealing with one angel, as Zechariah and Mary did, must be difficult enough. An entire army belting out the mighty works of God would have been overwhelming! Who knows how long it took them to recover themselves? I imagine that, after the heavenly army disappeared, it took some time. But after a long interval or a short one, the shepherds talk about their vision and together decide that they must go to Bethlehem, to see for themselves the facts behind the wonderful announcement.

As the second part opens, the scene changes again, from the fields back to the stable. Even though Luke indicates that the journey from the fields to the town is a long one, his narrative compresses the time to an instant. The shepherds hurried and found Mary, then Joseph, and finally the infant Jesus. Notice that Mary is again at the center of attention and action, with everything revolving around her. Indeed, the image preserved in so many Christmas card nativities—of Mary as the focal point, Joseph in the background, the infant Jesus in the foreground and the shepherds and various animals portrayed as onlookers—is, I think, fundamentally accurate.

What the Christmas cards fail to represent, however, is just how noisy this scene is. Having found Mary, Joseph, and the child, the shepherds immediately begin to talk about it both in the stable and throughout the town. Everyone who hears the shepherds' story, says Luke, is amazed. He leaves us with the impression both that the shepherds couldn't stop talking and that their audience was large. As they returned to their fields they announced to all who could hear what they had heard and seen. What an uproar!

And in the midst of the hubbub, Mary kept all these things and pondered or considered them in her heart. At the center of all the exuberance is silence—a silence so deep that it's beyond interpretation. Luke points to it, but doesn't explain it. While Mary's own fear yielded to confident assent (her "let it be" of Luke 1:38) and Elizabeth's blessing provoked Mary to sing the Magnificat's poetic praise (Luke 1:46–55), now Mary simply and silently weighs all these things. Luke never tells us just what these things are. I think he wants us to assume that they include not only the shepherds' visit, but everything else that's happened over the last forty weeks. It's been quite a time— an angel, a prophecy, a birth, and an audience. No wonder Mary is silent. But what does her silent pondering mean? Luke doesn't say. He leaves a gap and invites us to bridge it.

But before we do, let's look briefly at a second story that we'll examine more closely in the next chapter. It's the story of Jesus in the temple—the only narrative of Jesus' childhood in the New Testament. It opens with the explanation that when Jesus was twelve, his parents went to Jerusalem for the Passover, as they did every year. But on their way home, Jesus stayed behind in Jerusalem without his parents' knowledge. Down the road apiece, having discovered that Jesus wasn't among friends or family in the traveling party, his parents rushed back to Jerusalem where they frantically searched for him for three days. To their great relief, they finally found him safe and sound in the temple, conversing with the teachers there. Mary reprimands Jesus, Jesus appears to respond defiantly, and the family returns to Nazareth.

There are a whole host of problems with this story, but I'll highlight just two. First, what are we to do—especially if we're traditional Christians—with the notion that Mary would rebuke the Son of God? She'd seen an angel, heard the angel's announcement of her son's destiny, and embraced that destiny as her own. She'd even heard the shepherd's tale. Shouldn't she have expected, we might be tempted to ask, that strange events such as this one were bound to occur? After living with God's Son for twelve years, didn't Mary get it? Shouldn't she have been a little less harsh at the temple? I've heard all these questions from exasperated parishioners, and they're absolutely the right questions to ask, if not of me, then certainly of Luke.

Second, why is this story so clumsy? Till now, Luke's narrative has been almost seamless, with one event flowing into the next. Then, all of a sudden, twelve years pass in three verses and a strange tale that looks more like a legend than anything else is seemingly stuck in. Critical biblical scholarship, with its preoccupation with the historical construction of the text, has tended to write this part of Luke's narrative off as a later tradition awkwardly added to the original Gospel. While there's absolutely nothing wrong with being preoccupied by textual origins, and while there's no doubt that this story had a life of its own before Luke incorporated it into his Gospel, we can't let such interests distract us from the most important questions.

What is this tale doing here? How is Luke using it? These are the questions that pious and critical readers may, because of their different agendas and worries, overlook. But they're by far the most interesting questions of all. To answer them, we must move to the story's end.

After the rather awkward and abrupt conversation between Jesus and Mary, the boy joins his parents, leaves the temple, and returns to

Nazareth where he grows and matures. Of course, these words don't stand alone, for Luke uses them to tell us not only about the boy Jesus, but also about his mother. He ends this story just as he ends the birth story, telling readers that, while his parents didn't understand what Jesus was up to, Mary "kept all these things in her heart." With this little phrase, Luke ties the single story from Jesus' childhood to the scene at the manger. These are stories about Jesus *and* Mary: Jesus being born, Jesus doing the will of his Father, and Mary keeping all these things.

What is Mary doing? To answer this question is to enter a hole in Luke's story into which several possible answers fit. One straightforward answer highlights Mary's memory. In keeping these things in her heart, she is merely retaining what's happened in order to pass these things on to future generations. And according to some early commentators, Luke was the vehicle through which such passing on has taken place. The unique vocabulary and style of the first two chapters of his Gospel, coupled with his comment that Mary kept these things, has led some to conclude that Mary herself is the source for these opening chapters. They grant us deep insight into Mary because Mary is, in fact, their author.

More recent scholarship has exposed overwhelming textual and historical problems with this traditional interpretation. Most scholars today agree that even in his first two chapters, Luke is working with a variety of older sources, not with just one. And while it's possible that one of his historical records may well be—or at least be rooted in—what we could call "Mary's Memoirs," too much time has passed between the events and their recording for Mary herself to be Luke's witness. At the earliest, Luke's Gospel finds its final form around the year 80, by which time Mary would have been well into her late nineties. This is an age rare enough in our day; it would have been absolutely unheard of for a first-century woman. The sentimentally evocative image of an aged Mary dictating her story to a young scribe may well fire the pious imagination, but it squares neither with our understanding of Luke's text, nor with our understanding of the history of that text.

And when we read these stories closely, Luke's stress on Mary's keeping and pondering seems to have little to do with keeping a mental list or a chronicle for posterity. The conclusion to the second story seems to give us a different picture. As the Holy Family leaves Jerusalem, Luke tells his readers that although Mary and Joseph didn't understand Jesus' words, Mary kept them. And that brings up two important points. First, Joseph is completely eclipsed—this is the last we see of him. While we don't know his fate—whether he lived or died shortly thereafter—Luke implies that the breach between (earthly) father and son that occurred at the temple was never healed. Joseph didn't keep Jesus' words. Only Mary did. And in doing this, she was alone.

Second, notice that the focus of Mary's pondering isn't the past (Mary remembered these events in order to pass them on to us), but the future (Mary remembered them in order to come to a greater understanding of their significance). In the journey back to Nazareth, in the days and months that followed as Jesus came under his parents' authority, over the years as Jesus matured, Mary kept her son's words in her heart. The beautiful image that emerges is one of Mary watching her son, all the while reflecting, pondering, knitting, narrating, hoping to make sense of all the things she sees and hears as the future gives way to the past.

This is an image that's true to Luke's Gospel, strengthened when we look at the vocabulary of the two passages. In the first story, we're told that Mary "pondered" these things as she kept them (Luke 2:19). The Greek word translated here is *symballein*, which suggests combining, or bringing different ideas together. In the Septuagint, the Greek version of the Hebrew Bible that was the first Christian Old Testament, the word has prophetic overtones. Joseph, for example, interpreted the dream of the baker in prison by "pondering" it (Gen 40).

Perhaps Mary's silence is in some sense "prophetic," not in the sense of predicting the future, but in showing her dependence on God to interpret God's will correctly.

In silence, Mary put the details about Gabriel's message, Elizabeth's blessing, her own song, the census, the trip to Bethlehem, the manger, and the angelic appearance to the shepherds together. In dependence on God, she came to see in these events the unfolding plan of God for her and for her child.

Next, consider the phrase "kept these things," which arises in both stories (in 2:19 and 2:51). We'll get our bearings if we first look at how this phrase is used in the Septuagint. Consider two examples, turning first again to the Joseph story during the time before he was sold as a slave. After Joseph boasted to his brothers of his dream of the wheat sheaves, implying that they'd one day be his servants, their father, Jacob "kept this saying in mind" (Gen 37:10–11). While Joseph incurred the jealousy of his brothers, his father apparently weighed his words, or regarded them with concern, for they seemed to offer an omen about the future.

The second example is found toward the end of the Old Testament, in the book of Daniel. Again, the context is that of a dream that held great significance for the future and whose interpretation depended on a prophet specially enlightened by God. Daniel 4:28 tells us that after King Nebuchadnezzar heard Daniel's interpretation of the dream about the tree, "he kept the words in his heart." The details of the dream and its meaning aren't relevant now, but the image of a pagan king concerned by what he's heard in a conversation with the prophet is.

Looking at these other stories helps us understand Mary's silence. But let's make one more stop. To make sense of Mary's reaction, we must not only look for parallels in the Old Testament, we must also see how it stacks up against the way the shepherds and the temple onlookers reacted. The shepherds hurried to the manger, then began immediately to talk about what they'd seen. And both they and their hearers were amazed. Likewise, the witnesses to the temple exchange were also amazed by Jesus' wisdom. But only Mary hung on to her memories of the words and events and puzzled over their deeper meaning. Everyone else, having talked about it, apparently forgot.

Mary silently keeps; Mary silently ponders. And now, we understand just what Mary is up to both at the manger and at the temple. When Luke combines keeping the words with pondering them, we're meant to understand that Mary has preserved in her heart the mysterious words and events that surrounded Jesus' birth and his discovery in the temple, trying to interpret them. She didn't grasp the significance of all that she saw and heard, and she didn't entirely understand what was going on around, in, and through her and her Son. But rather than despair of making sense of it all, she listened willingly, and instead of talking, she chose not to speak until she understood. She allowed the words and events to sink into her memory and as Jesus grew and matured before her eyes, she sought to discern their meaning.

The conclusion of the stories of Jesus' birth and childhood show us that Mary's relationship to Jesus is symbiotic—mutually dependent. Jesus is growing in maturity physically and in his relationships with God and with other people. And in all of these things, he is dependent upon the care of his mother. Similarly Mary is also growing in maturity as a disciple, seeking to understand God's plan and God's will. And in all of these things, she's dependent on her Son.

Perhaps this is why Mary is the only character of the infancy narratives—apart from Jesus and John—whose stage presence continues further into the Gospel. Luke isn't primarily interested in her as an eyewitness or as a composer of memoirs; he's interested in her as a model of Christian discipleship. Her reaction in the annunciation narrative is one of humility, acceptance, and obedience. But complete discipleship isn't possible until the word of God has been proclaimed in its fullness—and that fullness comes, of course, only after the resurrection of the Lord.

As Luke will tell readers, some of Jesus' own followers who heard the word of God during Jesus' earthly ministry were unable to hold it fast; they abandoned Jesus as he was betrayed, sentenced, and crucified. Had it not been for divine help and strength, they'd never have returned. Mary is no exception—we'll see in the next chapter that the prophet Simeon will foretell that a sword will pierce Mary's soul. She won't be spared—her discipleship will also be tested. Will her commendable attitude of "keeping these things, puzzling over them in her heart" be enough when the sword of judgment comes? That's a question we can now raise, but can't yet answer.

For now, let's focus on what Luke is saying to us. While Mary has humbly accepted and obeyed, complete acceptance and full understanding are not yet possible. But Luke doesn't leave Mary in a morass of misunderstanding. She hasn't accepted and obeyed not because she *couldn't* grasp the plan of God, but because she *hasn't yet* understood. But, Luke implies, throughout the events of her life, Mary continues her search for understanding.

It's a search Luke calls us to emulate. Mary's journey to the cross and after begins with a divine call, as does ours. It continues with humble acceptance and obedience, as does ours. But Mary neither accepts nor obeys because God gives her a well-worked-out plan beforehand, in which the meaning of these events is outlined, plotted, and made crystal clear from day one. On the contrary: she believes not because God lets her in on a secret, but because she's confident that God will bring about what he's promised.

Her acceptance and obedience don't depend on a divine guarantee of absolute certainty, but on a confidence in the character of the One who called. In the meantime, there are things she just doesn't get. There are things that are amazing and unclear. And where others are quick to talk about them and then, presumably leave them behind as they exit Luke's stage, Mary keeps them. She ponders them in silence. She puzzles over them even as she continues to trust in God.

So it is for all who follow Jesus. At points in our journey to the cross with Jesus, the road ahead and behind will be clear and the painful tasks of mortifying and vivifying will at least be endurable, because they will seem to fit into a larger plan, because they will make sense in some way. Human beings can undergo tremendous physical, emotional, and mental suffering if they can see in it a purpose or see beyond it to a clear end. They can embrace incredible hardship if they can fit it into a larger rational framework. But it won't always be so. Sometimes we won't understand. Events will conspire from time to time to render the future uncertain, hidden, perhaps even utterly irrational. There will be no overall plan that will help us rationalize and endure our suffering. Sometimes God will seem to have forgotten us, or to have placed us in situations for which there's no evident explanation, which seem to serve no purpose, whether long or short term, human or divine. What will we do then?

I think here of a graduate of the seminary where I teach. A native Cambodian, he survived the killing fields by pretending to be dead after being hit over the head with a shovel. As the bodies of his parents and siblings were dumped on top of and around him in a makeshift mass grave, he swore revenge on the murderers of his family. He knew exactly who they were for they were his neighbors. He literally crawled out of his grave and, through a fascinating journey, eventually escaped Cambodia and immigrated to Canada. Here, he found personal and political stability that he'd never known before.

He also discovered that Jesus Christ had already found him—and not only found him, but called him to forswear his oath of vengeance and leave the security of his new home. Jesus called this victim of horrendous, violent political evil to take the gospel back to Cambodia, back to a land that was once his home, to a people who had rejected him, wished him dead, and acted to make that wish come true. He could have rejected that calling. And had he done so, none of us really could have blamed him. He was going back to an uncertain and probably hostile reception. Why not stay where he and his family would be safe? Where the killing fields would remain a very painful, but increasingly distant, memory?

He didn't stay in Canada. As I write, he's in Cambodia where he works as a Christian pastor and evangelist. Having read his letters to my college and seminary community, it is clear he has no idea what the future holds. And amazingly, he's perfectly content. He'll continue in silence to keep all these things—his own life story, his own encounter with Jesus, his own call to discipleship—in his heart. He'll continue in silence to ponder the significance of terrible events. He knows only that the future is in God's hands.

All of us will have to navigate this treacherous stretch of the Christian journey at some point, even if not in such a dramatic way. Some of us may have undergone it in the past while others may be doing it even today. Some of us right now may, having once trusted in God's gracious call, be utterly baffled at where that obedience has taken us. And we are weighing in the balance whether to continue on our journey with Jesus.

Wherever we are in our journey, Mary seems to suggest to us all that the way through such times is to persist with and in them, not forsaking the way of discipleship, but, however partially or incompletely, to continue to trust in God even as we keep these events in our hearts, puzzling over them, seeking to discover their meaning.

Almighty God,
you are Lord of our past, our present,
and our future.

Grant that as we search for signs of your Spirit's guidance,
we would, like Mary, entrust our future
to your care.

This we pray
in Jesus' name.
Amen.

For Reflection and Discussion

1. Luke pays close attention to the politics of Jesus' birth story. One reason is to anchor the story in history. What are some other reasons? In what ways might these reasons help us to think through our relationship as Christians to political structures whether local, state or provincial, or federal?

2. The image of an angelic army —rather than a choir—singing the Gloria to the terrified shepherds may be a new one for some readers. Does it cause you to read the story of the shepherds differently? If so, in what ways?

3. In the picture of Mary keeping these things in her heart, Luke offers us an image of discipleship as a work in progress. In what ways might growth in understanding challenge or deepen or fit within your own faith journey?

4. Mary's growth in understanding is also tied to her silence. What role(s) might silent reflection play in your faith journey?

5. On the other hand, talking in amazement seems to be tied to forgetfulness. Have there been points in your faith journey where you've talked too much? If so, what can you do to cultivate a more reflective, silent approach to faith in which you can ponder these things?

6. Luke presents us with a very realistic portrait of discipleship. Sometimes, he implies, it won't make sense. Sometimes God will seem remote if not completely absent. Have you experienced such times? How did you respond? Does Mary's response inspire, challenge, frustrate, or even anger you? Why?

A Sword Shall Pierce Your Heart

The Mystery of Struggle

LUKE 2: 22–40

*And Simeon blessed them, and said unto
Mary his mother, Behold, this child is set for the fall
and rising again of many in Israel; and for a sign
which shall be spoken against; (Yea, a sword
shall pierce your own soul also,) that the
thoughts of many hearts should be revealed.*
(Luke 2:34–35, KJV)

In the first two chapters of his Gospel, Luke paints three overlapping pictures of Mary. The first is the Mary of the annunciation and Magnificat, the Mary of the first four chapters of this book. Making her appearance in Luke 1:27, she's the most central character. She confidently assents to the will of God, and Elizabeth calls her blessed among women because she received the Word of God in her heart and in her womb. She and none other will be mother of the Lord. We hear Mary herself singing God's praises, calling to mind the way God keeps his promises, reminding both God and God's people that the lowly will be exalted and the rich sent away empty. She does and says all of this before Jesus is even born. In this Mary we see three central doctrines of Christian faith not resolved as much as set before us.

The first, the doctrine of divine election, teaches that God's grace isn't grounded in anything but God. God's favor can be neither earned nor unearned. It's a gift, not a wage. This doesn't mean that God's grace is arbitrary or capricious or grudging. God as disclosed in the man Jesus Christ is none of those things. Rather, it means that grace isn't grounded in us. God's gracious announcement through the angel Gabriel doesn't depend on any inherent quality of piety or virtue in the Blessed Virgin Mary. It rests only on God's insistence that he will be gracious. It's this grace—this unearned favor—that not only identifies, but also chooses and equips Mary the teenager to become the Blessed Virgin, the Mother of God.

So when we apply these titles to her in our reflection and in our worship, as it is surely right to do, we don't exalt her beyond her son, our Savior and hers. Rather, these titles accentuate that Mary's salvation and ours is the result of a divine call that neither Mary nor we can dictate, manage, or control. Grace is sovereign and free and overwhelming, for it is, simply, who God is. The doctrine of election doesn't conjure up the horrible image of a hidden God randomly choosing those on whom favor should rest. This God is not at all the God of Jesus Christ, the God of the Gospel. The doctrine of election reminds us that the God of Jesus Christ, the God of the Gospel, can't be controlled by any other. Like C. S. Lewis's lion in his *Chronicles of Narnia*, Aslan, God is not tame. God is good.

In spite of this emphasis on divine freedom and divine grace, Luke doesn't present Mary as a mere puppet in God's plan. Mary's freedom isn't nullified. For the second doctrine set before us in the annunciation is human freedom. The mystery that informs us that Mary is most fully herself, most fully in command of her own destiny when she affirms the angel's words, assents to the divine call, and embraces slavery to the Lord, is that she defines and embodies freedom by doing these things. If she's God's slave, she'll be no one else's——not even her husband, Joseph's. This understanding of freedom is certainly not that of the culture of the postmodern West. But that doesn't mean it's any less real. Indeed, those who take Mary's freedom most seriously soon find out that the "freedom" portrayed by *The Truman Show* is perhaps the most insidious form of slavery.

As it is for Mary, so it is with us——we're most fully ourselves, most free, only when we find ourselves enslaved to God. There's no room in Christian faith for freedom defined as neutrality. We'll be enslaved; the question is to whom. Will we be enslaved to those habits and desires, social structures and systems that seem to take on a life of their own, a life that the New Testament calls demonic? Or will we be enslaved to God, our true end, the one for whom we were created and the one in whom we are truly free? Behold God's slave, says Mary, and she points not only to herself but to us as well.

Third, as she who believed, Mary sets before us the ultimate harmony of divine grace and human freedom. Her story describes the sheer gratuity of the divine favor as one that irresistibly invites a free response of incredible trust in spite of the facts. For Mary, the facts were straightforward. She was pregnant by one other than her betrothed. She had to leave town for the Judean countryside. She may well have been regarded as delusional or demonized by her family and friends. After all, people in the first century conversed with angels about as often as they do today. Which is to say, about as often as virgins become pregnant.

There's no reason to doubt that because of her trust in God's favor, Mary had become an object of both scorn and pity in her community. And as such she's blessed. She's blessed because of the child she'll bear, who is in himself the sign of God's favor. She's blessed because, in spite of the facts, she stubbornly clings to her confidence in God's character, who would work his will in this situation regardless of how it looked. And Mary elicits from us a similar confident commitment. Will we, in spite of how things look or where our path leads, continue to trust in the One who has called?

In the birth story, a different Mary emerges. In Luke chapter 2, Mary's centrality is underscored by her unique silence. In the midst of the hubbub around the manger, she doesn't reveal to the shepherds—or even Joseph, for that matter—what she's been told by the angel and by Elizabeth. She merely takes the shepherd story of angelic armies singing God's praises, adds it to the strange and wonderful events that have marked her life for the last forty weeks, and treasures and ponders them in her heart. Only Mary, "kept these things and treasured them in her heart." Only Mary held on to the words, puzzling over their deeper meaning and trying to knit them into a single unified story. Just as Jesus is growing physically and relationally with God and others, Mary is also growing as a believer. Far from having full-blown knowledge of God's plan for her and for God's world, she must keep in her heart all the things that she and Joseph do not yet understand in the hope that one day, all things will become clear.

Until now, Mary's story has been pregnant—I use the word deliberately—with divine providence and promise. God's presence is so palpable at times that imaginative readers can sometimes, like Moses of old, catch a glimpse of God's back. God is there, but fleetingly, always just one step ahead, just outside the reach of our peripheral vision. And for many of us, our faith journeys begin in this same way. With a rush of excitement, God seems just around every corner, just behind the next building, lurking just beyond where our senses can take us. And God is waiting there, to surprise us with grace and truth and loving kindness.

In the church tradition in which I was raised, spiritual experiences in which the veil separating divine and the mundane seemed to thin to near transparency are highly prized and are at times presented as the norm for Christian life, or at least that life when it is truly and fully embraced. Because of that upbringing, I find it easy to enter into Mary's story as it begins to unfold. In many ways, it reads like those of the "saints" whom I read about and longed to pattern myself after, especially John and Charles Wesley and their friend George Whitefield.

But now the tone of Mary's story changes. The visible brilliance and rich harmonies of angelic choirs are shrouded and silenced. Luke's words depict a darker, more somber, and even painful picture as God, it seems, leaves. Once the central character, surrounded by angels and knowing family members, Mary is increasingly abandoned and marginalized. The angels depart to heaven, never to be heard from again. Elizabeth, after her blessing, drops entirely off the page without so much as a goodbye. Even Joseph, who nobly embraced the social stigma of Mary's unwed pregnancy to confer legitimacy on both her and Jesus, soon will not be heard from again. Mary herself speaks only once more. Does this mean Mary slowly falls out of the story? Not quite. Beginning in Luke 2:21, as her role diminishes, a third dimension of her character comes to the fore. And that's the aspect that will carry us to the end of the book.

According to Scripture, Mary goes with her firstborn son to the temple where she'll undergo ritual purification and he'll be circumcised and receive his name, Jesus. There, they encounter Simeon, a devout old man. Granted prophetic insight into the meeting's significance, Simeon praises God for allowing him to see in this infant a light for the Gentiles and the glory of Israel. So far, so good: we're still caught up in the wondrous story of the announcement and recognition of the Messiah, the Savior. And I'm sure we can imagine the joy with which Mary heard Simeon's blessing and the care with which she included his words alongside those of Gabriel, Elizabeth, and the awestruck shepherds.

But Simeon isn't done speaking. Still inspired by the Holy Spirit, his utterance becomes ominous. Turning away from Jesus, he fixes his gaze on the still silent Mary and foretells the destinies of both Mother and Son: "This child is destined to cause the falling and rising of many in Israel, and to be a sign that will be spoken against, so that the thoughts of many hearts will be revealed. And a sword will pierce your own soul too."

The last few weeks in Mary's life had been full of divine interventions: angelic announcements, prophetic proclamations. But now, a note of grief: a sword will pierce Mary's soul before this is all over. What is this sword? If we can come to understand this most difficult of metaphors, then we will come to understand Mary and our own journeys of discipleship better.

The first inkling of just what it might mean comes in the next story, recounted in Luke 2:41–52. We've moved ahead only a few verses, but in Luke's Gospel some twelve years have elapsed. The baby is now a boy on the verge of manhood. As was their habit, Joseph and Mary have journeyed to Jerusalem for the Passover. On the way home, they discover that Jesus is missing. Frantically, they search among their friends, slowly working their way back through the caravan to the place where their journey home had started: in Jerusalem. Jesus is eventually found in the temple courts, debating and questioning the teachers of the Law. All, says Luke, were amazed at his ability to engage the teachers with a level of understanding well beyond his years.

All save his mother, who quite understandably rebukes her son: "Child, why have you treated us like this? Look, your father and I have been searching for you in great anxiety." To which Jesus replied, "Why were you searching for me? Did you not know that I must be in my Father's house?" Some readers may fault Mary for rebuking her son—it shows, they might say, just how much she misunderstood Jesus, just how much she didn't believe. It should have been obvious to her that Jesus, about to become a son of the Torah, would take this opportunity to signal his true identity by naming his true father; not Joseph, but God. She should have known.

I don't think that's fair. Indeed, any parent who has had a child wander away in a shopping mall, whether for ten seconds or ten minutes, should know the anguish and worry that framed Mary's rebuke of her son. Jesus was lost! Who knows what had happened? Mary certainly didn't. And like any good parent she prayed to God that the worst hadn't happened as she searched, looking for some sign, some shred of hope that the boy Jesus was safe. In her question we see the heart of an anguished mother.

My frustration doesn't lie with Mary. If anything, it lies with Jesus! His answer is in no way a response to his mother's almost desperate question. Indeed, it looks like a rejection of her right to even ask such a question. More than that, we can't say. Mary didn't entirely understand his words, but added them to those memories that she treasured. For us, however, they should be clear: Jesus' understanding of family was radically different from his mother's. Even though he was her son, her flesh and blood, Jesus makes it all too clear that he did not belong to her and that his mission could not and would never be constrained by the natural bonds of motherly affection. She both was and was not his mother. And this was going to be a source of great pain. At the temple, Simeon's sword was drawn from its sheath.

The nature of that pain is elaborated in two more passages coming much later in the Gospel. The first is Luke 8:19–21. There, Luke tells us that Jesus' mother and brothers were prevented from seeing him because of the crush of the crowd. When this is brought to Jesus' attention, he responds ambiguously: "My mother and my brothers are those who hear the word of God and do it."

Readers are left puzzled. Does Jesus mean that his mother and siblings are to be numbered among his disciples because they hear and practice God's commands? The grammar certainly allows this reading of the passage. On the other hand, does it mean that Jesus' true family is to be distinguished from his physical family, made up not by blood, but by obedience? The structure of the story, with the deliberate placing of Jesus' family on the outside, seems to indicate this. The text is ambiguous.

And that, I think, is Luke's point. At one level, the meaning of Jesus' words is obvious. They're perfectly clear that for Jesus, family relationships are not the way most of the rest of us understand them. It is clear that as far as he's concerned, his family is defined not by bloodline, but by obedience to the one he called Father. At another level, they hide and obscure far more than they communicate. "What about Mary?" "What about the brothers and sisters?" they invite us to ask. But the answer isn't forthcoming. It's not at all clear whether Mary or sisters or brothers are inside or outside the scope of Jesus' true family any longer. Simeon's sword has been placed at Mary's breast.

Third, the same tension is found in Luke 11:27–28. Mary doesn't appear here, but she's blessed by an unnamed woman who cried out to Jesus, "Blessed is the womb that bore you and the breasts that nursed you." We ought not to be surprised that such words were spoken of Jesus. After all, they recall and may well be a fulfillment of Mary's own prophetic words in the Magnificat: "From now on, all generations will call me blessed."

The anonymous woman's blessing tells us nothing about Mary. Both it and the Magnificat to which it alludes are designed to move our focus through Mary in order to settle it on Jesus and his greatness. Mary is there. She is involved. But she comes into view only as the recipient of God's gracious blessing.

Now, some of us might expect that Jesus' reply would support this reading of the text. A commendation of this anonymous woman for honoring Jesus' mother is what we expect. But Luke's Jesus far more often defies expectations than fulfills them. Far from comforting, Jesus' response highlights and even accentuates the ambiguity that seems to define his relationship to his mother.

When he says, "blessed are those who hear and keep the word of God," does he mean that Mary is indeed blessed not by her biological relationship but by her obedient discipleship? Like the previous

passage, there's nothing in the grammar of the verse to rule this reading out. It's possible. It's also possible, however, that Jesus is contrasting his physical and true families again. Being Jesus' blood is no
guarantee of divine favor. Only those who hear and obey in Jesus'
mind are blessed. Jesus again leaves us wondering whether Mary is
numbered among the disciples, the blessed ones or not. All we can say
for certain is that Jesus' understanding of family is very different from
simple blood ties.

We can say with confidence that Simeon's sword has indeed
pierced Mary's soul for from this point, Mary drops out of the Gospel
altogether. Having already surrendered her speaking role, she now is
no longer present, even as a shadow of the past. As Jesus moves
toward the climax of his ministry, he does so alone, without his
mother. Tellingly, as Luke's Gospel ends, Mary is neither at the cross
nor a witness to the resurrection. Her final relationship to Jesus is
never clarified in the Gospel.

Simeon's prophecy had to do with the judgment that would come
upon the people of Israel with the coming of Jesus. Many would rise
and fall with his coming. Many thoughts would be exposed. The
sword of judgment that would pass through the land of Palestine,
Simeon says, would also pass through Mary. No one would be spared
from the divine judgment that Jesus embodied. Nobody, as far as Luke
is concerned, is automatically "in." Not even Jesus' mother.

The sword Simeon prophesied, the sword that pierced Mary's
heart, was the threat of exclusion from God's kingdom. It was the
recognition, even from the time of the temple, that Jesus' role and
mission would inevitably sever what is perhaps the closest relationship
in the human family—that of mother to child. He was her son. Flesh
of her flesh. Her humanity was the only humanity he knew. And yet,
her dreams were not his. Her doubts were not his. It's not clear
whether she belongs or not. Luke leaves us wondering whether Mary
really is on the inside—among those who hear the word of God and

obey it—or on the outside among those who see but do not perceive and who hear but do not understand.

Is she in or out? Is she part of Jesus' true family or not? These questions—which Luke himself invites readers to ask through his brilliant story-telling—are left hanging. And in the silence, we can shift from Mary's world to our own. Or better, we can begin to understand our own discipleship in the light of hers.

Were we to leave Mary in the Christmas chapters, hearing the words of the angel and pondering the words of the shepherds, were we to leave her smiling her Mona Lisa smile, were we to leave her in silent contemplation, we might be left with the notion that she has been "in on it" from the start. We might be left wondering whether she really is an example for us or not. After all, what kind of example believes God from the beginning, never doubts, never wavers, never wonders just who Jesus is or what his mission means?

No, Luke's Mary is an example for us precisely *because* she's so much like us. At times, her relationship with Jesus is clear and obvious. What room for doubt is there when you're talking to an angel? Just so, there are times in our lives when we can't be more certain of our relationship with God in Christ. We're confident of God's care for us and we won't be dissuaded. And at times, Mary's relationship to Jesus isn't at all clear. Is she blessed or not? Is she among the obedient or not? We don't know, and she may not know, whether she fits in Jesus' plans or not. And there are times in our lives when we don't know about ourselves. We can point to times when we were certain; we can remember times when we were certain about our relationship with God, but somehow things have changed. For whatever reason, we've been left wondering where or whether we fit into Jesus' plans.

Perhaps you find yourself there today. You don't know whether you're a disciple. You're clear that you're not on the outside. You're clear that you hear the word of God and you do your best to obey it. But Jesus—he seems remote. He seems surrounded by the needs of others. He seems to be working more in others' lives than in your own.

Perhaps you feel that while you're not really out, well, you're not really in, either. If I've described your situation, take heart for you have in Mary, the mother of God, an accessible example who lived through a troubled and ambiguous time that may have lasted some twenty years.

That kind of struggle is, of course, quite foreign to us today. We're surrounded by self-help books by self-help gurus containing self-help strategies that promise ultimate happiness with minimal effort. Jesus' way isn't like that. Jesus said his way was narrow, that his road was difficult and led to the cross. And Lent is a penitential time when we come to grips with just how difficult this road can be from time to time. It's a time when we discern just how far we have to go in the long road of sanctification—of learning to die with Christ in order that we might live with him. And we will, from time to time, be tempted to find a way more appealing, easier.

Jesus, of course, doesn't want us to give up in despair. But he doesn't bolster our confidence by giving us cheery slogans or sure-fire tactics that enable us to retain our happiness or avoid spiritual struggle altogether. What Jesus has done is to leave us, through the Gospel of Luke, the example of his mother. She too went through times of frustration, struggle, and doubt. No disciple has it easy. And while that won't right every wrong, in the midst of the worst of them, it is enough.

Lord Jesus Christ,
in grace you have called us to follow you
in the way of the cross.

Strengthen us through the example of your mother,
who felt the sword of your judgment
more keenly than any.

This we pray
through your holy name.
Amen.

For Reflection and Discussion

1. In this chapter, we encountered a new Mary—one who struggled to discern just what her relationship to Jesus was. How does her experience compare with yours? What does her life show you about Christian discipleship? In what ways does the Mary of the Passion make the Mary of the annunciation seem more accessible or more remote?

2. Simeon's prophecy contains both a promise of blessing and a promise of judgment—not just for Mary, but for all Israel. How does this promise affect us as modern followers of Jesus? What do Simeon's words of blessing mean to you in your life? What about his pronouncement of divine judgment?

3. How do you encounter the sword of judgment that the coming of Jesus brings? Is the metaphor even appropriate anymore, or has our human history of violence put it beyond use?

4. The story of Jesus at the temple embodies every parent's worst nightmare: a lost child. How do you hear Mary's question? Is it a rebuke? A cry of anguish or anger? Why? How do you hear Jesus' response? Is it appropriate, insolent, obvious? Why?

5. In your opinion, do Jesus' remarks on his "true" family deliberately include Mary because of her obedience or exclude her because of her disobedience? In what ways is your perception of Mary's discipleship influenced by your perception of her relationship to Jesus?

6. How does Mary's pilgrimage resemble your own? What reflections does Mary's experience of ambiguity invite for you?

At the Foot of the Cross
The Mystery of Faithfulness

JOHN 19:1–42

Now there stood by the cross of Jesus his mother,
and his mother's sister, Mary the wife of Cleophas,
and Mary Magdalene. When Jesus therefore saw his mother,
and the disciple standing by, whom he loved, he saith
unto this mother, Woman, behold thy son! Then saith
he to the disciple, Behold thy mother! And from that hour
that disciple took her unto his own home. After this,
Jesus [knew] that all things were now accomplished. . . .
(John 19:25–28a, KJV)

Jesus' "hour" has come.

Jesus first mentioned his hour at his first miracle, the turning of the water into wine (John 2:1–12). When his mother came to him to tell him that the wedding party was running low on wine, he responded with words notoriously difficult to translate. Usually, they run along these lines: "What does that have to do with you or me, woman? My hour is not yet come." Of course, what looks to us like a rather rude rebuff was not. Jesus does fix the problem. His miracle produces the very best wine and the party can continue.

The story concludes that the disciples saw this display of Jesus' glory and they believed in him. Not anymore, it seems. Even though Jesus has been alluding to the coming of his hour constantly since John 12, the disciples seem to be awfully dull. And when the hour comes—when he's nailed hand and foot to the cross—they all forsake him and run away. All, that is, except four women and one man, the disciple whom he loved.

The presence of the mother at the cross, at the end, ought to remind us of her presence at the wedding, at the beginning. John wants us to think about Jesus' words, "my hour is not yet come," (John 2:4) again. He wants his readers to understand that the hour that was not yet is now here. The hour symbolically portrayed in the story of the transformation of water into wine now crushes in upon us with the terrible weight of historical reality. The hour, Jesus' hour, is the hour of his death.

This is the hour when the Son of Man will be lifted up from the earth; the hour when he will enter into his glory, the glory of the One and only Son of the Father; the hour when he will draw all people to himself. This is the hour of the great messianic banquet, when the new wine will be poured out, better than all that had come before.

Here's an example of John's irony at its sharpest. The hour foreshadowed in the first of Jesus signs, the hour of the messianic banquet, the hour of the wedding party, the hour when the new wine would be provided as a gift of sheer and radical divine generosity, was here. In the Place of the Skull. On a cross, where a Jewish man was suspended by ropes and nails. This was the hour to which the symbolic wedding-wine had pointed all along. John invites us here to see in the midst of the suffering and filth and humiliation, the One and only Son in his messianic glory, full of grace and truth, completing his mission and securing for you and for me that new relationship with God, his father, that we may be able to participate in God's wedding banquet at the end.

And, near the cross, John tells us stood the mother of Jesus. She was there at the beginning of his ministry; she is here at the end. Why? What role does she play? Is there more going on here than a simple narration of history? We'll look at these questions in a moment.

First, let's look closely at the Scripture itself. Notice first how John contrasts the behavior of the four soldiers with the behavior of the four women. The soldiers' story begins in verse 23. John portrays them as off to one side, talking among themselves, dividing the clothes of the now naked Jesus into four piles—one for each of them. This seems like a trivial detail—four piles for four soldiers, but its significance will become clear in a moment. They come to the last piece of clothing, Jesus' undershirt, and decide to gamble for it so it won't be torn up.

John says this is a fulfillment of Psalm 22:18, ". . . for my clothing, they cast lots" (John 19:24). It's interesting to note that while the crucifixion stories in Matthew and Mark are different in many ways from that of John, all three make reference to Psalm 22. This is a song of divine abandonment, a plea for divine intervention. Would God intervene on Jesus' behalf at the coming of the hour? No. The four male soldiers are busy sorting the spoils, what little they were, stolen from this dying Jew. The four women, on the other hand, stand still and silent. They are transfixed; immobilized by the terrible scene unfolding in front of them. Jesus will not be rescued. Those at the cross can't or won't help.

Second, pay attention to the women. John gives them to us in two pairs. The first pair are unnamed members of Jesus' family: specifically, his mother and his aunt. The second pair—who have no family relationship—are named: Mary of Clopas and Mary the Magdalene. Neither Jesus' aunt nor Mary of Clopas appear anywhere else in this Gospel, though tradition has long maintained that Jesus' aunt is Salome and Mary of Clopas is the wife of the disciple Cleopas, mentioned in Luke 24:18. Mary Magdalene is introduced here for the first time in John's Gospel, and she'll figure prominently in chapter 20, in the account of the resurrection.

John likely leaves the members of Jesus' family anonymous to underscore that what he understands as important about them is contained in their relatedness to Jesus. Because Jesus has a mother and an aunt, we can say that he's no divine imposter, masquerading as a human being. He's as fully human as you and me and there, on the cross, he's really dying.

Third, having introduced the four women, John again turns his attention to Jesus. First Jesus sees and then he speaks. He sees his mother and the disciple whom he loved. So, apparently, the women were not alone. The disciple whom Jesus loved was there, too. The disciple whom Jesus loved is first mentioned at the meal that marks the beginning of the Passion Narrative in John chapter 13. He's probably the anonymous disciple who follows Jesus into the high priest's courtyard, highlighting thereby the cowardice of Peter who remains outside in chapter 18.

Of all the disciples, only he stands near the cross with the women. When Mary Magdalene tells of the resurrection, he races with Peter and arrives at the tomb first. And we read at the conclusion of the Gospel that it's this Beloved Disciple who composed this Gospel. His presence seems to mark every turning point in the second half of the Gospel.

But when Jesus speaks, he turns first to his mother. "Woman," the simple designation, again reminds readers of the wedding in John chapter 2 and the symbolic significance of Jesus' first miracle. Having caught her attention, Jesus adds, "Behold your son." And she, I expect, turns her gaze one last time to the one whom she bore some thirty years before. To look at him one last time. But Jesus' words are not an invitation to look upon him. For Jesus speaks again, this time to his Beloved Disciple: "Behold your mother."

With these words, Jesus creates a new mother-son relationship. At one level, this is a perfectly natural and human thing to do. As the

oldest son, presumably without full brothers or sisters, the responsibility for the care of his mother fell solely to Jesus. And his last action
is to initiate a form of adoption by which his mother will be looked
after. No longer will she be regarded as the mother of Jesus. From
here on, she'll be the mother of the Beloved Disciple. Similarly, no
longer will the Beloved Disciple be the beloved of Jesus, but of his
mother. Jesus entrusts them to each other.

"And from that hour," John tells us, "this disciple took her into his
home." The new family bond is established. Jesus no longer has father
or mother; he faces the climax of his ministry alone. Suspended
between heaven and earth.

But even as he does so, a new, earthly relationship is established
between the anonymous Beloved Disciple (only later tradition tells us
that it is John), and the unnamed mother of Jesus. This is the last act
of Jesus' life. For John tells us in verse 28 that by initiating this new
relationship, Jesus had completed everything.

So much for the story. What are we to make of it? On the surface,
this last of Jesus' actions is John's way of disclosing to us just how
much he loved his mother and a sign of his humanity. He saw her, he
recognized her need, and, as at the wedding in Cana, he met it. Certainly this is the case. This is the way John, so far as I can tell, intends
his readers to understand the story at the first level.

On a deeper symbolic level, Jesus is about to depart, to return to his
Father. Before he does, he has one more task to accomplish. He
entrusts his mother to his disciple, and his disciple to his mother. I
believe John is talking here about the Church's relationship to the apostles' teaching. On the one hand, all who would receive the salvation
Jesus brings (symbolized by the mother of Jesus) must come under the
care of those who knew Jesus best, the apostles (symbolized by the
Beloved Disciple). Of course, the apostles are now gone. But their
memories of Jesus, their understanding of his significance, remain.

They've been preserved for us in the Bible. First, their Bible, the
Old Testament, and second, their memories, their understanding of

how this man, Jesus of Nazareth, unlocked for them the meaning of their Bible. In the New Testament, we have the words of the closest followers of Jesus explaining to subsequent generations just who Jesus is and what his life, death, and resurrection accomplish. Just as Mary was given to John, so Jesus gives the Church to his apostles for ongoing guidance.

But Jesus also gives the Beloved Disciple to his mother. Reading Mary as symbolic of the Church and the Beloved Disciple as symbolic of the apostles works equally well with this second half of Jesus' command. For the apostles' teachings are cared for, preserved, protected, and indeed understood nowhere other than the Church. The corporate body of all those who long for the Lord and his appearing, who want to see the gift of salvation that he brings, gathered together constitute the community that reads and seeks to understand this book. These teachings, the very ones through which we have indirect access to Jesus himself.

Here the story becomes relevant for us today. For it can and should be read as both a warning and a promise to all of us. First, as a warning, it suggests the dangers of approaching the teaching of the apostles apart from the churchly context to which they were given and in which they may be understood. More to the point, it speaks profoundly against the dangers of a "Jesus and me" spirituality that forsakes the communion of fellow-believers across time and space for its own esoteric or idiosyncratic or just plain weird biblical interpretation. It's a profound warning to those of us who emphasize a personal, individual relationship with God through Christ. That's not wrong, but such an individual relationship needs to come under the guidance and discipline of Holy Scripture as it is read corporately by the body of Christ—the church.

Evangelical Protestant Christians—and I am one—have a particularly nasty habit of thinking that because all Christians have a personal, individual relationship with God through Christ, that all opinions about biblical interpretation, theology, and Christian ethics are equally valuable, equally true. I hear such sentiments fairly often from some of my students. And every time I do, I want to say that's the same as saying that everyone who has a driver's license therefore knows as much about cars as a mechanic. No! Becoming a Christian doesn't automatically make one an expert in discerning the meaning of the apostles' teaching. It means that one now may submit oneself to the teaching of those whom the Church has set aside as expert readers. And even the experts are themselves bound to the consensus of the Church as a whole. As an individual believer, you are incorporated into the Church and the Church stands under the teaching of the apostles. We are not free as individuals to make the Bible say what we want.

Finally, this story is also a promise, from Jesus himself to each of us who have been incorporated into the Church through our baptism. He is gone, but he has not left us without guidance. He's given us into the care of the apostles, and through them given us a full and complete disclosure of who he is and how he has reconciled us to God. When we gather together to hear their teaching read and proclaimed, we're granted access to Jesus himself. For, as John himself put it, "these are written so that you may come to believe that Jesus is the Messiah, the Son of God, and that through believing you may have life in his name" (John 20:31).

Lord Jesus Christ,
In dying you created a new family:
your church led by your apostles.

May we, like Mary,
entrust ourselves to their guidance.
May we, like her,
be sure safe guardians of their witness.

This we ask
in your name,
Amen.

For Reflection and Discussion

1. John seems to want us to read the death of Jesus through the lenses of the Cana wedding. Why do you suppose he does so? What difference does it make when you do?

2. The whole description of the crucifixion seems to emphasize Jesus' powerlessness and his abandonment. What does this image of the powerless, abandoned, suffering Jesus present to you?

3. John presents the death of Jesus as the way in which Jesus creates new family bonds, not simply between his mother and his disciple, but bonds that extend to today in the church. What do you think of his understanding?

4. Jesus has entrusted his church to the care of his apostles. The meditation suggested one way in which this care may be understood. Is that interpretation convincing? Why or why not?

5. Are there other, in your mind, more persuasive ways of understanding the story of Jesus, his mother, and his Beloved Disciple? What makes them better readings?

In the Upper Room
The Mystery of Perseverance
ACTS 1:1–14

These all continued with one accord in prayer
and supplication, with the women, and Mary
the mother of Jesus, and with his brethren.
(Acts 1:14, KJV)

Our journey with Mary has come to an end. We've walked with her from the Annunciation through the Judean countryside to Elizabeth's house. We've journeyed with her from Nazareth to Bethlehem. We have traveled with her to Jerusalem, three times: once to hear Simeon's warning, once to search for Jesus in the temple, and once to watch Jesus die. We've seen a life marked by angelic visitations, prophetic proclamations, extraordinary faithfulness, and everyday ambiguity. And now at last, we arrive with Mary in the upper room. It's a good place to leave her. For now, finally, her place as our model is clear.

She's a model of discipleship not because she heard an angel, or because she agreed to God's will, or because she was a prophet. She's a model disciple because she persevered. Because she kept her faith in moments of keen spiritual insight and in moments of dull darkness. She persevered through the humiliation of an unwed pregnancy. She persevered through what appears to be a troubled relationship with Jesus. She persevered through the judgment of God foretold by old Simeon. She persevered through the disaster of the cross. She persevered to become a founding mother of that new community created by her son's death and resurrection. She endured.

The journey of Lent, and the journey of the entire Christian life, is a marathon, not a sprint. It's one in which the greatest demand is for perseverance. We thank God that he left us an example of holy endurance in the Mother of his Son. Her Savior and ours.